1 MONTH OF FREE READING

at
www.ForgottenBooks.com

By purchasing this book you are eligible for one month membership to ForgottenBooks.com, giving you unlimited access to our entire collection of over 1,000,000 titles via our web site and mobile apps.

To claim your free month visit: www.forgottenbooks.com/free447529

* Offer is valid for 45 days from date of purchase. Terms and conditions apply.

ISBN 978-0-484-29067-8
PIBN 10447529

This book is a reproduction of an important historical work. Forgotten Books uses state-of-the-art technology to digitally reconstruct the work, preserving the original format whilst repairing imperfections present in the aged copy. In rare cases, an imperfection in the original, such as a blemish or missing page, may be replicated in our edition. We do, however, repair the vast majority of imperfections successfully; any imperfections that remain are intentionally left to preserve the state of such historical works.

Forgotten Books is a registered trademark of FB &c Ltd.
Copyright © 2018 FB &c Ltd.
FB &c Ltd, Dalton House, 60 Windsor Avenue, London, SW19 2RR.
Company number 08720141. Registered in England and Wales.

For support please visit www.forgottenbooks.com

ALFRED THE GREAT;
OR, THE PATRIOT KING.
AN HISTORICAL PLAY, IN FIVE ACTS—BY JAMES S. KNOWLES.

Dramatis Personæ. [See page 20.

As performed at the Theatre Royal, Drury Lane, 1831.

ENGLISH.			DANES.	
ALFRED, (King of England)	Mr. Macready.	SOLDIER		Mr. Dowsing.
ODDUNE	Mr. J. Vining.	ELSWITH, (The Queen)		Miss Huddart.
OSWITH	Mr. H. Wallack.	MAUDE		Mrs. C. Jones.
EDRIC	Mr. Younge.	GUTHRUM		Mr. Cooper.
EGBERT	Mr. Thompson.	AMUND		Mr. Bland.
KENRIC	Mr. Cooke.	OSCAR		Mr. C. Jones.
EDWY	Mr. Sinclair.	HALDANE		Mr. Howard.
OSWALD	Mr. Cathie.	OTHO		Mr. Yarnold.
ARTHUR	Mr. Eaton.	SOLDIER		Mr. Howell.
EDGAR	Mr. Honner.	PRIEST		Mr. S. James.
EDWIN	Mr. Fenton.	BOY		Mr. Fenton.
CONRAD	Mr. Hammerton.	INA, (Guthrum's Daughter)	Miss Philips.
ETHELRED	Miss Marshall.	EDITH		Miss Faucit.

No. 314. Dicks' Standard Plays.

COSTUME.

SAXONS.

ALFRED.—1st. *Dress*: Plain brown swineherd's shirt, flesh leggings and arms—sandals—bonnet. 2nd *Dress*: Disguise large brown mantle, similar to a minstrel's habit of the period, with hood attached. 3rd *Dress*: Long yellow cloth shirt, richly trimmed with gold—blue robe or mantle—plain gold coronet.

OSWITH.—Heavy suit of chain mail, flesh arms and legs—helmet, shield, axe, and sword—low russet boots with spangled tops.

EDRIC.—The same style.

ODDUNE.—White shirt, fleshings, sandals—bonnets with steel embroidered bands.

THE OTHER CHIEFS.—Similar in colour and of equal quality.

ELSWITH.—Faded double dress, ragged drapery, long hair, sandals.

MAUDE.—Blue stuff dress with hanging sleeves trimmed with red—long hair—blue fillet.

DANES.

GUTHRUM.—Long purple cloth shirt, bullion trimming—square yellow robe fastened with brooch in front of the neck—plain gold crown—gold staff.

OSCAR.—Armour legs and arms, richly embroidered surcoat—helmet and shield.

HALDANE.—Shirt richly trimmed with gold—breastplate and red mantle.

DANISH CHIEFS.—Red shirts, brass or steel breastplates, and helmets silver, with a raven—axes—short cloaks, buskins, shields, and light spears.

INA.—Green Danish robe and amber long embroidered train trimmed with white, short hanging sleeves, and white under dress, trimmed with blue—long hair—sandals.

EDITH.—Plain classic dress drapery—long hair—fillet—sandals.

THE DANES.—All armour.

THE SAXONS.—White shirts and fleshings.

STAGE DIRECTIONS.

EXITS AND ENTRANCES.—R. means *Right*; L. *Left*; D. F. Door in Flat; R. D. *Right Door*; L. D. *Left Door*; S. E. *Second Entrance*; U. E. *Upper Entrance*; M. D. *Middle Door*; L. U. E. *Left Upper Entrance*; R. U. E. *Right Upper Entrance*; L. S. E. *Left Second Entrance* P. S. *Prompt Side*; O. P. *Opposite Prompt*.

RELATIVE POSITIONS.—R. means *Right*; L. *Left*; C. *Centre*; R. C. *Right of Centre*; L. C. *Left of Centre*.

   R. RC. C. LC. L.

*_** The Reader is supposed to be on the Stage, facing the Audience.
*_** The lines marked with inverted commas omitted in the representation.

ALFRED THE GREAT.

ACT I.

SCENE I.—*The Danish Camp.*

Enter EDITH *with a bow and quiver, followed by* INA, 1. E. R. H., *attended by a boy, who carries a bow and quiver.*

Edith. Come, let us see who'll hit the target first?
Ina. My bow hath got a cast, and will not shoot.
Edith. In sooth, your bow hath got no cast at all,
'Tis true as mine. Take mine—I'll shoot with it.
Ina. Your's fits me not—'tis harder far to draw.
Edith. Try it.
Ina. No, no; I will not shoot to-day.
Besides, my arrows all have lost the nock.
Edith. Here's store enough of mine.
Ina. Good Edith, no;
Entreat me not—I will not shoot to-day
Edith. Why, so 'twas yesterday; fie, Ina, fie,!
To tax thy bow with fault it never had.
Thy bow that hath a cast is thy chang'd will,
The nockless shafts are marr'd alone by that.
You wont to love this sport; from morn till night
Your pastime 'twas, and now you love it not!
What love you, sweet, instead?
Ina. What should I love?
Edith. Nay, Ina—you alone can answer that.
Has Otho's suit prevail'd?
Ina. When did a flower
Spring from a weed, that love should grow from hate!
Edith. What! call you love a flower? A flower looks gay—
So looks not love! A flower is sweet—who says
That love is sweet? Does sweetness garner pain
For those that own it? Rather love's a weed
Oft taken for a flower—found out at last
With a sigh! O, Ina, you have pluck'd this weed!
Come, own it, Ina!
Ina. Wherefore do you look
Thus at me?   (*Crossing to* P. S.)
Edith. Why do you, my Ina, look
At anything but me? Why do your eyes
Of late their lustre lavish on the ground,
That cares not for it? And your honey'd breath,
That should be given to your silver tongue
To make rich music of, why do you waste
Oftener on thankless and contentless sighs?
Come, tell me, Ina, what has happen'd to you?
Ina. Alas! I know not.
Edith. Do you say alas!
O, then 'tis over with you! Why, you're in tears;
Only the drop's but half-way out, that soon
Would make way for the rest, held not your eye
Its crystal door upon it! Lean your head
Upon the bosom of your friend, and give
Your secret vent—for sure you have one, Ina!
Ina. Not I!—Come, take your bow!—I'll shoot with you!
My quiver 'gainst a shaft, I'll be the first
To hit the mark. Set up the target, boy!
           [*Exit Boy,* 1. E. L. H.
Now for the eye of the eye. In sooth I've miss'd
Wide by a mile—but thou hast shot full home!
I've pluck'd it, Edith, flower or weed. If weed,
Oh! weed most like a flower.—Oh precious weed!
There's not a flower so fair, I'd deem thee graced
To call thee by its name!

BOY. (*Running in.* 1. E. L. H.)

The battle's won! The battle's won!
I see our troops come winding up the glen,
Their spears and banners wreath'd,—a token sure
Of victory.
                  [*Exit,* L. H.
Edith. Let's meet them, Ina:—Come!
Why sweet, what's this? How pale you turn!
How damp's
Your little hand! Nay, 'tis snow indeed.
Cold as 'tis white! Did you not rightly hear?
He says the battle's won!
Ina. I know he does.
Edith. Is't with such cheeks you listen to such news?
This would become a daughter of the foe.
Ina. The foe! The foe!
Edith. What! find'st thou something sweet
In that harsh word, that thou repeat'st it thus?
Ina. Harsh word! now, harsh art thou to call it so;
Jars it thine ear? there's music in't to mine.
Stands it for what thoud'st shun? that's what I'd seek;
Yea! 'fore the things that brother, sister, friend—
Soft titles—stand for: Ina loves a foe;
That foe has lost the battle we have won.
Edith. Why sweet, where sawest thou this gentle foe?
Ina. Even here. When last the Saxon ask'd a truce,
Curious to see their herald, I remain'd
Behind you in my father's tent. He came!
Oh, with what grace of richest manhood! Proud
His gait, yet bearing onwards looks so bland
As made all hearts give willing way to him.
He spake, and I took root to where I stood,
And so did all. Not Guthrum moved; Oh Edith!
How should it be with Ina? Where were her eyes?
What were her ears about? What did her heart?
Dost feel it throbbing now? 'Tis quiet now
To what 'twas then! How often have you tried
To *fix* your naked eye upon the *sun*:
And when you've ta'en it *off*, how has the *day*,

From gazing his bright face, been turn'd to *night*
Flowers, verdure, darken'd; yea, the orb *himself*
From *burning gold*, grown *ink*. 'Twas so with *me*;
When sight or him was gone! Night turn'd to day
Again with *you*—but light's gone out with Ina
E'er since the day she look'd upon her foe!
                                  (*Crosses* R. H.)
    Edith. Hence, Ina hence awhile; your father
        comes!
He must find looks of welcome.
    Ina. Have with you.
You've won my secret, Edith! Guard it for me.
                                  [*Exeunt*, R. H.

Enter GUTHRUM, AMUND, OSCAR, HALDANE,
    and Danes. U. E. L. H.

    Guth. Halt, comrades, halt! and change your
        toil for rest,
And then from rest to feasting! We'll carouse
A moon for this last victory, that leaves
No future foe to front us. England's won;
                                  (*Shout*.)
So thinned her sons by this last overthrow,
And utterly discomfited, enow
Remain her not to make another stand
Durst Alfred rally them—their throneless king!
" We shall not need to cross the main again
" To prop us with fresh succours. Here we'll build
" Another Danish kingdom, fairer far
" Than what we've left. What ho, there! bring
    me wine;
I'm thirsty from our march. Ho! wine, I say!
A seat! Here, in the open air, we'll drink,
Or ere we part, to our new Denmark. Chief
And followers shall pledge me. Wine I say!

Enter OTHO, U. E. L. H.

    Otho. Guthrum, your priests prepare a sacrifice,
The God expects his victims, shall he have them?
    Guth. Take them! You know the God must have
        his due!
                        [*Exit* Otho U. E. L. H.
Give him the wine! my thirst's gone off—yet, no;
'Tis fit that I drink first (*drinks*.) To our new
    Denmark!
By Odin! 'twas a glorious victory!
The God deserves his victims—he shall have them!
Odin's the God of war! If he drinks blood,
He has a right. Who dares deny the God
His victims? Amund, take the cup! We fought
Like Odin's sons. I saw you, Amund, cleave
In twain a Saxon at a single blow.
    Am. My Lord, 'twas slight to what your falchion
        did,
" That thro' the casqued head and mailed chine
" Made way at one dire wheel!
" Guth. Ay, did it so?
" I do believe it did!" No more of that.
Give me your hand, good Amund—for that blow
Lord of a gallant castle shalt thou be.
Pass on the cup to Oscar. (*Crosses to Oscar*,) Oscar!
    ha!
Show me thy falchion's edge—Look, Amund,
    here—
I saw him keep at once five Saxon swords
At bay! Well done!—(*Crosses back to seat*)—Oscar,
    be sure you sit
On my right hand at banquet.
    Osc. Mighty chief.
" I mark'd your eye was on me; 'twas a sword
" That more than balanced all the odds against me!

" Besides, your arm just then had turn'd the fight
" That seem'd at first against us."
" Guth. Was it so?
" I don't remember it. Good Oscar, ask
" What portion of the spoil thou wilt—'tis thine!"

OTHO *re-enters*, U. E. L. H.

    Otho. The victims, chief, are ready.
    Guth. So! enough!
    Otho. Eight of them did we take by lot,—the
        ninth
Is self-devoted to preserve the life
Of one, to whom we were about to hold
The fatal urn.
    Guth. Indeed! a chief?
    Otho. The port
Of both bespeaks them men of proud degree.
    Guth. Have 'em before us; we would see them.
                        [*Exit* Otho., U. E. L. H
Guthrum
Loves war! He'd leave the banquet any time
To mingle in the fight. He loves a friend;
But more than friend's embrace, he loves the hug
Foe gives to foe. Yet is not Guthrum cruel;
His foe disarm'd he never yet could smite.
He loves a noble deed, altho' the sword
Achieves it not. How say you friends, wer't right
To save the man, who loves his friend so well,
He lays down life for him—altho' a gift
To Odin?
    Osc. Ere the priest his sacred hand
Lays on the victim, it has still been lawful
To snatch him from his doom!
    Hal. Behoves him tho'
To swear eternal league with Odin's sons.
    Guth. He'll do it, Haldane! Ha! I saw thee
        matched
In fight, for once. That Saxon found thee, Hal-
    dane,
With two that back'd thee, livelier work than suits
A sluggard's hand. Thy seconds both were down.
Was't not so, Haldane? And thyself, methinks,
Mad'st rather backward way, when I despatched
Fresh aid to thee, with charge, at any risk,
To take thy gallant foe alive. 'Twas you,
Oscar, that I so charged.
    Osc. My liege, he lives;
O'ercome by force that could not make him yield,
But bore him down to earth, where, as he lay,
The strife his fettered limbs caused him to drop;
His eye continued still, that shot around
Deadly defiance in the face of death.
    Guth. " Foe worthy Guthrum's sword." Was't
        not the herald,
Last sent us from the English King?
    Osc. The same.
    Guth. I'd like to see that man again.
    Osc. He's here!

Enter OTHO, *with* OSWITH *and* EDRIC *chained*,
        U. E. L. H.

    Guth. This he!—Men's looks reflect their deeds
        as well
As natures. One of these is he, whose thought
Of lofty friendship overlooks himself,
When fix'd on his friend's need—This is the man!
    Otho. It is, my Lord.
    Guth. Is he thy friend, whose life
Thou count'st a thing so precious, that would'st
    give
Thine own to purchase it?

Os. He is.
Guth. What rich
And heavy debt hast thou incurr'd to him,
To pay so large return as takes thy all?
Os. And think'st thou friendship barters kindnesses?
'Tis not because that such or such a time
He help'd my purse, or stood me thus or thus
Instead, that I go bound for him, or take
His quarrel up! With friends, all services
Are ever gifts, that glad the donor most.
Who rates them otherwise, he only takes
The face of friend to mask a usurer.
I give my life for him, not for the service
He did me yesterday, or any day,
But for the love I bear him every day,
Nor ask if he returns!
Guth. Be Guthrum's friend.
Thou livest, and thy friend for sake of thee.
Edr. O, generous proffer!
Os. Would'st accept it?
Edr. Yes.
Os. Then do.
Guth. Remove their chains.
Os. First take off his.
Guth. Now thine!
Os. Long as my country wears your chains,
Guthrum beware how you unrivet mine!
For once you set my arm at liberty,
The thing which first 'twill seek will be a sword,
To right my master, royal Alfred's cause—
And strike my injured country's fetters off!
Guth. Saxon, beware! The smooth and gentle tide
Of mercy thwarted, turns a torrent, oft
O'erwhelming as the raging flood itself
Of vengeance.
Os. Here I stand—let it come down!
I care not when or where its fury rushes!

Enter INA *and* EDITH, (*as yet unperceived by* GUTHRUM, &c.) 2. E. R. H.

Ina. (*Aside to Edith.*) 'Tis he!
Guth. Is Guthrum braved!—Is he the son
Of Odin!—Marches in his van the God
Of War!—Lies o'er the humbled necks of hosts
Of prostrate foes his path; and brooks he thus
Defiance, and from one earth sprung—the spawn
Of the vile clod he treads on? Stood thy King
Alfred, of whom thou vaunting spok'st, stood he
Where now thou stand'st, his regal eye had fallen
Beneath the frown of Guthrum.
Os. Not beneath
The frown of Guthrum's god, were Odin real
As he is fabled!
Guth. Give him to the God!
Ina. Father!
Guth. My Ina!
Os. Ha! could I believe
He was not born of earth—there were, indeed,
An argument could make me.
Guth. I have given thee
Thy choice of life or death—thou choosest death,
And take it.
Ina. Father.
Guth Ah, thou ever art
My sweet and welcome calm, that glads me, sunlike,
When summer days are breathless with the joy
Of his enriching beam. I'm smooth again!
Not a ruffle! not a ruffle! Is he not gone? Hence with him!

Ina. No, no, my father!
Guth. Would'st thou have me set
A foam again?—Nay, Ina, if I rage,
'Tis not at thee!—Why start away from me?
Come back, and cling to me again! close, close!—
My child, belov'd and only, tell me, if
Thou can'st, how much I love thee!
Otho. Saxon, come.
Ina. No, no!
Guth. How, Ina?
Ina. Thou did'st not repeat
Thy order.
Guth. But I will.
Ina. Oh, speak to me!—
I'm glad the fight is o'er. You won it soon!
You won it safely, else it were not won!
How stood the plume I fasten'd on your crest?
Well, well! How many eyes were on that plume,
Tossing, as proud it rode the stormy wave
Of battle, still the more majestical
The fiercer wax'd the swell!
Guth. My child, my child!
Aye, every inch my own When thou wast born,
I wish'd a son. I would not give thee now
For troops of them!—What, Otho!—
"*Ina.* Your scarf! It's whole?
"No, no, a rent is here. Come, take it off.
"False as it is, you shall not wear't again!
"I'll knit you another, every loop of which
"I'll fasten with a spell, that it shall prove
"An amulet against the thrust of spear,
"Or stroke of falchion!
"*Guth.* So you shall. You make
"A child of your father! Otho!"
Ina. Not a wound!
For ever in the thickest of the fight,
And not a wound! Thank Odin! Yet I would
There were a slight one—for the tending on't!
No, no! and yet in sooth I would there were!
I know not what I say! I prate! I prate!
Thank Odin, You are safe!
Guth. My girl! my girl!
My idle girl! my foolish, loving child!
My Ina! What! and have I won the fight,
And shalt not thou become the richer for't?
By Odin, bu thou shalt! Come, ask me something.
Name me some gift. Come, measure, if thou canst,
Thy father's love for thee! What wilt thou ask?
Ask me a kingdom! Come?
Ina. No kingdom, father.
I'd ask of thee—only one little boon.
Guth. What is't? Speak out!
Ina. Is't granted?
Guth. By the God!
Out with't—What is't? What little boon is this
Which only wants the naming, to be thine,
And yet thou seems't to lack the breath to name.
"*Ina.* Is that a rivet of your armour broke?
"No, no!
"*Guth.* And if it were, no blame to it.
"It turn'd an English javelin. At my feet
"The weapon fell: I snatch'd it up again,
"And sent it hissing at its master's head;"

Enter SOLDIER, U. E. L. H.

Soldier. This packet, found we, Guthrum, in the tent
Of Alfred.
Guth. Bring'st no tidings of himself?

'Tis certain that he left the field unhurt!
Have they return'd whom in pursuit of him—
  Soldier. They have. Three days they track'd
    him; on the fourth
All trace of him was lost; but, by report,
Alone—without a single follower,
The royal fugitive pursues his way,
Broken in hopes, as fortunes.
  Guth. We may chance
To overtake, or light upon him yet.
Give me the paper.

  (*Takes the packet, and reads. Crosses to*
    R. H. *Corner.*)

  Os. Such things I have heard of—angel forms
Enchantment raises—mocking fairest things
Of earth, but fairer—to entrance earth's sons—
"Things they would deem of heaven, tho' found
    on earth!"
Which, once beheld, their helpless functions seize
With ravishment, that leaves them but the power
To gaze or listen, till no warning effort
Of reason, or stronger will avails, to tear
The charmed sense away!
  Edr. Would I were chained
Again! Her pity makes rich freedom poor,
That can't awaken it.
  Guth. (*Throws away packet*). It matters not
A string of Saxon rhymes. Can Alfred fight?
Who flourishes the pen so much, can scarce
Be master of the sword! He plays the harp,
So they report. The harp! Give me the strain
Of the resounding shield! (*Crosses to her*). Come,
    Ina, name
The boon thoud'st ask.
  Ina. When thou art happy, what
Most wishest thou?
  Guth. That happiness may last.
  Ina. No, no! not that. Thou wishest others
    happy.
  Guth. I do! I do!
  Ina. And so do I. When I
Am happy, I'd have all things like me—not
That live and move alone, but even such
As lack their faculties. Then could I weep,
That flowers should smile without perception of
The sweetness they discourse. Yea, into rocks
Would I infuse soft sense to fill them with
The spirit of sweet joy, that everything
Should thrill as I do. "Then, were I a queen,
" I'd portion out my realms among my friends,
" Unstud my crown for strangers, and my coffers
" Empty in purchasing from foes their frowns,
" Till I had bought them out; that all should be
" One reign of smiles around me." I am happy
To-day—to-day, that brings thee back to me,
The hundredth time, in triumph and in safety!
This day, that smiles so bounteous upon Ina,
She'd wish to smile e'en upon Ina's foe—
Let not the Saxon die!
  Guth. He lives!—My child!
What makes thee gasp?
  Ina. How near—how near to you
Was death that day. 'Twas well for Ina that
Your armour proved so true. She had not else
A father now to ask a boon of, and
To get it soon as ask'd!
  Guth. He lives thy slave!
Had he been wise, he now were Guthrum's friend.
  Ina. His chains——
  Guth. 'Tis thine to take them off or not.

What Guthrum gives, he gives! He is thy slave.
Come, Saxon, thou art free!
  [*Exeunt Guthrum and Chiefs*, 1st E.R.H.
  "Edr. Would I were chain'd
"Again.
      "[*Exit.*"
  Os. I gaze, and with my tranced eyes
Drink magic in. I know it, still I gaze.
And yet can bane reside in aught so sweet?
Can poison lodge in that consummate flower,
Which blends the virtues of all blooming things,
And with the wealth of its fair neighbourhood,
Enriches very barrenness, that near it
Grows sightly, e'en, and sweet?
  Ina. How's this, my Edith?
"My wish obtain'd, I tremble to enjoy;"
I need but speak the word, and he is free:
Yet, there I let him stand in shackles still,
Whose chains to doff, were there no other way,
I'd go in bonds myself.—"Sweet, be my tongue;
"Bid them" remove his chains.
  "Edith. Unbind him, there!
  "Soldier. My hand is useless, from the fight to-
    day.
  "Ina. Try you."
  Edith. (*Crossing to centre, trying to take off his
    chains.*) It baffles me! It hath a knack
I am not mistress of.—Will you not try?
  (*Ina approaches and takes off his chains.*)
You've done't.—Why, what's the matter with you,
    Ina?
Hast put his fetters on, that here you stand
As tho' bereft of motion? Rouse thee, Ina!
  Ina. O, for a minute, Edith, in thy bosom,
To weep there! Ay, to weep!—to shed such tears
As shower down smiling cheeks, when sudden joy
Pours in to the o'erfilling of the heart,
That look'd not for't, and knows not what to do
With all its treasure!
  Os. I do feel it still!
Still do I feel the touch of her fair hand!
How passing fair! The driven snow itself
Might make as white a one; but then, again,
As cold as that is glowing! Who will loose
The fetters it puts on? Or, who that wears them,
Would sigh for the embrace of liberty!
Truth! honour! all is laps'd. O, for a foe
To taunt me now!—O, for a flourish of
The Danish tramp—or would their banners come
And flout me!
  Ina. Saxon, will you follow us?
  Os. I come, sweet maid! What am I but your
    slave,
To follow, tho' I leave all else that's bright?
      [*Exeunt* 1.E.R.H.

END OF ACT I.

ACT II.

SCENE I.—*A wild tract of country on the border of
a wood.*

Enter ELSWITH, *in wretched attire, presently followed by* CONRAD.

  Con. No farther!
  Els. Yes!
  Con. Alas! I can no more.
My lapsed strength constrains my limbs to play
The traitor to you!
  Els. What! an thou fall off?

Well! I am left at last alone! Old man,
Think not that I'd upbraid thee. Thanks to thee
For what thou'st done, for what thou can'st not
  do
No blame to thee, but pity for thee! More
I know my desolation is thy loss
Than mine! back prithee to the hut we've left.
Thou hast strength enough to crawl there.
  Con. What I have
I'll turn to worthier profit. (*Makes a violent effort,
  and snatches hold of her robe.*) Oh! my
  lov'd,
My honour'd mistress! do not tempt these wilds,
Where hunger turns its aching eyes around
In ain! where prowls perchance the savage wolf!
Where——
  Els. Peace! talk terror to the dead! Not less
Would'st thou be heeded. I've a heart as dull,
Except one fear—one hope—to find my Alfred,
Or search for him in vain. There, I'm alive!
There only! Counsel should not come from thee,
Whose tongue persuaded what thy arm enforced,
Desertion of my child! whose fate to avert,
A mother's duty 'twas! or, else, to share!
And now thou'dst urge desertion of his sire!
" I wonder not thy limbs are weak—thy heart
"Not in the cause! and yet it is a King's!
" But thou'rt his subject only; I'm his wife—
"So doubly—trebly true." Back to the hut!
They'll take compassion on thee! Fare thee well!
  Con. Nay, pause in mercy; See who comes—
    alas!
Should they be Danes!—Yon thicket will conceal
  us—
For thy own safety!—come!—Alas, the help
I'd give, I stand myself in need of most!
                                   [*They retire.*

Enter KENRIC, ARTHUR, *and other Saxons.*

  Edwy. We've rounded now the forest on the
    East,
And by the sun our friends should meet us soon
Who gird the other side. A halt awhile.
  Arth. But should we meet the King—if still he
    lives
Nor yet is captured, as 'tis rumoured—he
May pass our band unknown; by none of us
Ever beheld except at distance, when
He marshalled us, to lead us 'gainst the foe.
                       (*Elswith rushes forward.*)
  Els. Seek ye your King?
  Edwy. Who art thou?
  Els. I'll be your leader
Until you find him!
  Arth. She's distracted.
  Edwy. Yes.
That can't be reason's light which shines so
    strong
In her unquiet eye—that misses nought,
Yet rests on nothing!
  Els. I command you Sirs,
On your allegiance follow me. Obey
Your Queen!
  Arth. Our Queen?
  Edwy. You mark! A Queen indeed,
If frenzy ever made one! Arthur, come,
Our friends will mock us, should they chance to
    reach
The point agreed upon before us.
                       [*Exeunt Edwy and party.*
  Els. Stay!

  Con. (*Appearing, and struggling to advance.*)
      Stay, countrymen! It is indeed your
        Queen
Alas! they hear me not! my tongue hath wax'd
As feeble as my limbs.
                              (*Leans against a tree.*)
  Els. Why let them go!
They are not half the band that I have here
In loyalty to my liege, wedded lord!
With that I'll seek him, under Heaven's high
    guard!
Yea, tho' I search the quarters of the foe!
In that find strength—find courage! That my
    food,
My rest! Farewell old man! Heaven shelter
    thee!
And be thy mistress's guide!
                                             [*Exit.*
  Con. Stay!—Hear me!—Stay!
I'll drag my limbs along to follow thee.
                                             [*Exit.*

SCENE II.—*A hut. Alfred discovered trimming
  some arrows, with an unfinished bow beside him.
  Maude kneading flour for cakes.*

  Maude. (*Aside.*) Ay! there he's at his work; if
    work that
Which spareth toil. He'll trim a shaft, or shape
A bow with any archer in the land,
But neither can he plough, nor sow!—I doubt
If he can dig—I am sure he cannot reap—
He has hands and arms, but not the use of them!
Corin!
  Alf. Your will?
  Maude. Would thou couldst do my will
As readily as ask it! Go to the door;
And look if Edwin comes. Dost see him?
  Alf. No.
  Maude. Bad omen that! He'll bring an empty
    creel;
Else were he home ere now. Put on more wood;
And lay the logs an end; you'll learn in time
To make a fire. Why, what a litter's there,
With trimming of your shafts that never hit!
Ten days ago you kill'd a sorry buck;
Since when your quiver have you emptied thrice,
Nor ruffled hair nor feather.
  Alf. If the game
Are scarce and shy, I cannot help it.
  Maude. Out!
Your aim I wot is shy; your labour scarce;
There's game enow, would'st thou but hunt for
    them;
And when you find them, hit them. What
    expect'st
To-day for dinner?
  Alf. What heaven sends!
  Maude. Suppose
It sends us nought?
  Alf. Its will be done!
  Maude. You'd starve;
So would not I, knew I to bend a bow,
Or cast a line. See if thou hast the skill
To watch these cakes, the while they toast.
  Alf. I'll do
My best.
  Maude. Nor much to brag of, when all's done!
                                             [*Exit.*

  Alf. (*Solus.*) This is the lesson of dependence.
Will

Thankless, that brings not profit!—labour spurn'd,
That sweats in vain; and patience tax'd the more
The more it bears. And taught unto a king—
Taught by a peasant's wife, whom fate hath made
Her sovereign's monitress. She little knows
At whom she rails; yet is the roof her own;
Nor does she play the house-wife grudgingly,
Give her her humour! So! How stands the account
'Twixt me and fortune?—We are wholly quits!—
She dress'd me—She has stripp'd me!—On a throne
She placed me—She has struck me from my seat!
Nor in the respect where sovereigns share alike
With those they rule, was she less kind to me—
Less cruel! High she filled for me the cup
Of bliss connubial—she has emptied it!
Parental love she set before me too,
And bade me banquet; scarce I tasted, ere
She snatch'd the feast away! My queen!—My child!—
Where are they? 'Neath the ashes of my castle;
I sat upon their tomb one day—one night!
Then first I felt the thraldom of despair.
The despot he! He would not let me weep!
There were the fountains of my tears as dry
As they had never flow'd! My heart did swell
To bursting; yet no sigh would he let forth
With vent to give it ease. There had I sat
And died—But Heaven a stronger tyrant sent—
Hunger—that wrench'd me from the other's grasp,
And dragged me hither!—This is not the lesson
I set myself to con!

Re-enter MAUDE.

Maude. 'Tis noon, and yet
No sign of Edwin! Dost thou mind thy task
Look to't! and when the cakes are fit to turn
Call, and I'll come!
Alf. I'll turn them, dame.
Maude. You will?
You'll break them!—Know I not your handy ways?
I would not suffer thee put finger to them!
Call, when 'tis time! You'll turn the cakes forsooth!
As likely thou could'st make the cakes as turn them!
 [*Exit.*

Alf. So much for poverty! Adversity's
The nurse for kings;—but then the palace gates
Are shut against her!—They would else have hearts
Of mercy oft'ner—gems not always dropp'd
In fortune's golden cup. What thought hath he
How hunger warpeth honesty, whose meal
Still waited on the hour? Can he perceive
How nakedness converts the kindly milk
Of nature into ice, to whom each change
Of season—yea, each shifting of the wind
Presents his fitting suit? Knows he the storm
That makes the valiant quail, who hears it only
Thro' the safe wall—its voice alone can pierce;
And there talks comfort to him with the tongue,
That bids without the shelterless despair?
Perhaps he marks the mountain wave, and smiles
So high it rolls!—while on its fellow hangs
The fainting seaman glaring down at death
In the deep trough below! I will extract
Riches from penury; from sufferings
Coin blessings; that if I assume again
The sceptre, I may be the more a king
By being more a man!

MAUDE *re-enters, goes towards the fire, lifts t cakes, goes to Alfred, and holds them to him.*

Maude. Is this your care?
Ne'er did you dream that meal was made of corn
Which is not grown until the earth be plough'd;
Which is not garner'd up until 'tis cut;
Which is not fit for use until 'tis ground;
Nor used then till kneaded into bread?
Ne'er knew you this? It seems you never did,
Else had you known the value of the bread;
Thought of the ploughman's toil; the reaper sweat;
The miller's labour; and the housewife's thrift;
And not have left my barley cakes to burn
To very cinders!
Alf. I forgot, good dame.
Maude. Forgot, good dame, forsooth! You ne'e forgot
To eat my barley cakes! (*Knock.*) Open th door!
 (*Maude sets the cakes on the table wher she had been kneading them; Alfre opens the door.*)
Alf. An aged man!
Maude. Come in!

Enter an OLD MAN.

What want you?
Old Man. Food!
Maude. Want calls on want when you look her for food!
Old Man. Good dame, to say I have not tasted food
Since morning yesterday, is not to speak
My need more urgent than it is
Maude. Whate'er
Thy need, we cannot administer to it—
Seek richer quarters.
Alf. Stay! He's in the gripe
Of straitest want. There's food, and give it him!
Maude. Ay, when we've scanty stock for three days more.
Alf. We breakfasted this morning; yester night
We supped, and noon ere then had seen us dine.
Since yester morn he has not touched a meal!
Whoe'er lacks food 'tis now his turn to eat.
This portion would be mine—I'll go without!
Here!—Here!—Good dame, the hand which gave us that
Will not more sparing be of its bounty be
For using thus its gift! The hand that fed
So many thousands with what only seem'd
Provision for a few, could also make
The remnant answer us for many a meal!
Old Man. Oh, strong in faith!—In mercy rich! Whoe'er
Thou art, that hand is with thee! Was't thou great,
And art thou now brought low? 'Twill make thy fall
Thy rise—thy want abundance—thy endurings
Enjoyings—and thy desolation, troops
Of friends, and lovers countless! Does the storm
Hold on? Ne'er heed it! There's the sun behind,
That with effulgence double shall break through,
And make thee cloudless day.
 [*Exit.*
Maude. A poor man's wish,
They say, is better than a rich man's gift.
If house and lands thou'st lost, I would not say

But thou may'st get them back again, with roof
enlarged and acres grown. Yet lands and house
To come, are not so good as bread in hand.
And that thou'st given away, if Edwin speeds
No better than he did yesterday!
  Alf. Ne'er fear—
These arrows when I've trimm'd, and strung this
    bow,
'll find thee out a garner in these wilds
To dress the table still!
  Maude. I'd rather trust
A peck of barley meal to furnish it!
  Edwin. (*Without.*) What, hoa! within!
  Maude. 'Tis Edwin's voice!
  Edwin. (*Without.*) Within!
Open the door!
  Maude. Thank Providence, his hands
Have something else to do!   [*Opens the door.*
  Edwin. (*Entering with a sack.*) Provision, wife!
A month's subsistence! Take it in, and ply
Thy housewifery; for friends must eat of it—
Guests sure of welcome who supply the board
They ask their hosts to spread. A gallant troop
Of countrymen, for common safely link'd,
And wand'ring thro' the land, with hopes, they
    say,
To learn some tidings of their king; and if
They find him, list themselves beneath his banner,
And face the Dane again!
                                  [*Exit Maude.*
  Alf. (*Aside.*) The land's not lost!
That's left a son to struggle for 't. The king.
Has yet his throne, that's firmly seated in
His people's hearts.
  Edwin. (*Going to the door.*) In! in!

Enter EGBERT, KENRICK, ARTHUR, EDWY,
  OSWY, *and others, variously armed.*

  Eg. Thanks, friend!
  Edwin. No thanks.
You're guests, the frugal'st host might entertain,
Who cater for yourselves. Sit down. The board
Shall soon be covered.
  Eg. And we have a cup
To cheer it with, with richer beverage
Than what the fountain yields, replenish'd. Bring
A flagon, worthy host—
  Ken. (*Aside to Arth.*) Commend him to
A cover'd board and brimming cup! He's fit
To play the leader there;—but he's no head
For men like us, that rise betimes for meat,
And wish for busy hands. I'm weary on't!
  Arth. (*Aside to Ken.*) And so am I! and trust me,
    of our minds
Are many more.
  Ken. To lead a life of shifts
That we may dine in safety! I'll no more on't!
Give me a skirmish!
  Arth. Tell him so.
  Ken. I will,
Ere I touch food again.   (*Returns with Arth.*)
  Eg. (*To Alf.*) Is it a bow
You shape?
  Alf. It is.
  Eg. I pray you show it me.
  Alf. (*Rising and coming forward.*) Here.
  Eg. (*Struck with the appearance of Alf.*) Forgive
me that I call'd you from your seat.
  Alf. No wrong is done where none is meant.
  Eg. You make
The wrong the greater, so excusing it.
Lodge you beneath this roof?
  Alf. I do.
  Eg. (*Aside.*) I've met
With men whose faces utter histories,
That seeing them I could tell their course of life—
Whether on ocean or on land—uneven.
Or smooth—almost what perils they had run,
Or incidents of happy fortune seen.
Now his is one of them.
  Alf. You'd see the bow?
  Eg. (*Mechanically taking, and almost at the same
    time returning it*). Your pardon.
                (*Alf. returns to his seat.*)

Enter MAUDE *with cakes, which she lays on the
table, while one of* EGBERT'S *party enters with a
flagon, and sets it down.*

  Maude. This bread will serve till more is ready,
    friends.   [*Exit.*
  Eg. Sit down.
  Ken. Sit down who will, I'll not sit down!
  Arth. Nor I.
  Osw. Nor I.
  Eg. Why? what's amiss?
  Ken. We loathe
To lead this wary life. The very deer
Confess the covert irksome, and at times
Betake them to the plain.
  Eg. Not when they hear
The hunters are abroad! Sit down! Sit down!
  Ken. We'll not sit down, till 'tis determined
    who
Shall head the table.
  Eg. I shall head it.
  Ken. Ay?
  Edwy. And wherefore should he not?
  Ken. Go to! Go to!
You question far too bold for one so young.
  Edwy. I question in the right, and so am bold
Far less than thou, that question'st in the wrong.
  Ken. The wrong? Thou'rt but a boy!
  Edwy. The boy that proves
Himself a man, does all a man can do.
  Ken. Beware thou dost not prove thyself on me,
My metal's temper'd—thine at best but raw.
Before thy chin exchanged its coat of down
For one of manlier fashion, I had shown
A beard in twenty fields.
  Eg. No more of this!
The post by lot is mine. I got it not
Of mine own choice; nor yet by partial leave.
It fell to me. It might have fallen to you,
To him, or him—to anyone—and then—
No matter! If, by fearing to be rash,
And overshoot the mark, my shaft hath lit
O'ershort on 't, I am content a better bow
Should lead the game.
  Edwy. It shall not be! We'll have
No other leader? Sides, sirs, sides!
  Ken. Come on!
When they've such stomach for 't, 'twere strange if
    we
Lack'd appetite. Come on!
  Alf. (*Rushing in between them as they are on the
    point of encountering*). Hold!! Stop!
    Which side's
The Dane? I stand for England! Can it be
You're Saxons all! What? Are your foes so few
You make ones of each other? Fie, sirs! Fie!
  Arth. (*To Ken*). Who's he?
  Ken. I know not.
  Alf. (*To Ken*). You're a soldier?

Ken. Yes.
Alf. Whose sword is that you draw?
Ken. My own.
Alf. Your country's!
You took it, with an oath to use it 'gainst
Her foes, and do you turn it on her sons?
For shame!
Arth. Why bear you his rebuke?
Alf. (*To Arth.*) And you?
Arth. A soldier too.
Alf. (*To Osw.*) And you?
Osw. The same.
Alf. Beneath whose banner shot you arrow last?
Arth. and Osw. The king's.
Alf. And take you aim at the king's liege?
As well the king himself! What! do you stand
With grasped weapons still? Or do you look
For signal here?—Old soldier, why is this?
Is't thus you use your battle-temper'd sword?
Is that the rust of Danish blood upon't?
These hacks—are they the thrusts of Danish
  blades?
Ne'er hath it met the foe that master'd it?
Ne'er hath it fail'd the friend that call'd upon it?
Still did it guard thy country while it could?
Yet would it back thy king, did he command?
And would'st thou tarnish it?
  (*Ken. hangs his head.*)
The field, the field,
You drew it last in?—ha! You start at that!
Remember you who won that field? You do!
His shout is in thine ear again! Thine eye
Beholds him scattering carnage thro' the ranks
Of those that fled!—The Saxon then was down!—
What! tighten you your grasp, till with the strain
Your weapon trembles? Keep it for the Dane,
And put it stainless up!
  (*Ken. sheathes his sword. Arth. and
  Osw. unbend their bows. The rest
  follow the example.*)

Eg. (*Aside*). What man is this,
That lacks all sign and title of command,
Yet all obey?
Edwy. We're friends again.
Ken. Content.
Eg. A cup, then, to our making up.—Sit down.—
A pledge for concord, friends—The king!
All. The King!
Eg. I pray you, Edwy, sing those rhymes for us,
You've strung so well, and we so love to hear.
Edwy. Right willingly; tho' homely be the
  verse,
I dare be sworn was ne'er more rich in heart
  (*Sings.*)

  When circling round the festive board
    The cup is fill'd the highest,
  And one and all their love record
    For him their thoughts the nighest—
  Who owns the name their lips pronounce,
  While vouching tear-drops spring, Sirs,
  In eyes he does not see? At once
    I'll tell you—Here's "The King," Sirs!

  When proud in arms the nation stood,
    To front the foul invader,
  And England did what England could,
    And fate alone betray'd her—
  Who was the foremost to advance,
    The first a spear to fling, Sirs,
  The last to quit the field? At once
    I'll tell you—Here's "The King," Sirs!

  And now, when o'er the prostrate land
    The spoiler roams resistless,
  And Vengeance fears to lift her brand,
    And Hope almost is listless—
  Whence does the beam of solace glance,
    The song of heart'ning ring, Sirs,
  And promise freedom yet? At once
    I'll tell you—Here's "The King," Sirs!

Eg. Well sung.
Edwy. What's well intended, scarce comes
  short,
Howe'er performance halts—I did my best.
Alf. My heart o'erflows!—I shall betray myself!
What could my palace boast to vie with this?
Not for its carved roof would I exchange
These rafters, 'neath whose shelter, vanquish'd,
  stripp'd
Of crown and sceptre, I am still a king—
My people's hearts my throne!
Eg. What trumpet's that?
Arth. (*Going to the door.*) I'll see.
Ken. I know.
Eg. Whose is it?
Ken. 'Tis the Dane's.
I know his flourish well. Let's out and meet
  him!
Is't not the Dane?
  (*To Arth., who returns.*)
Arth. It is. They're close upon us!—
A quick retreat!—Their numbers double ours.
  (*All start up except Alf.*)
Alf. No more?
Arth. No more!—What can we, one to two?
  (*Alf. rises, looks sternly at him for a
  moment, and exit, hastily, in an opposite direction.*)
Eg. Why goes he?
Arth. For his safety to provide.
Let us provide for ours by instant flight.
Ken. He's not the man to fly! My life upon it,
He'll never turn his back upon the foe!—
I told you so!
  (*Alf. returns, armed with a sword and target.*)
Alf. What distance off's the Dane?
Arth. Scarce half a mile by this.
Alf. (*To himself.*) The wood's to pass.
Unseen we can approach, and set upon them.
All unprepared for us. Divide your band!
  (*They mechanically obey him, alternately looking at each other and at Alfred, with an expression of wonder and inquiry.*)
Half with your leader go; and half with me!
  (*Eg. mechanically heads one of the divisions.*)
Ours be it to charge! They're sure to waver.
  Then
Our shout your signal be to second us!
My bounding heart presages victory!
And so I see does your's, old soldier Come,
There be our first trust; and our second here!
Say, would you back your king. Then follow
  him
  [*Exit Alfred, Eg., and the rest
  enthusiastically following.*

SCENE III.—*The Country, Interspersed with Wood.*

Enter ODDUNE, EDGAR, Chiefs, and Soldiers.
EDGAR bearing the standard of the *Rafen.*

Od. Halt, comrades   Here we'll take our noon's repast.

This velvet sward will be our pleasant couch,
To rest us from our toil. And lose not heart!
We'll find our Alfred yet! What though our search,
Has hitherto proved vain? When look'd for least
Perchance we'll light upon him. Fortune smiles,
Like fortune's frowns, when once they come, come thick.
Our expedition fairly has begun,
Fairly proceeded, and will fairly end.
 Edg. Know you these parts?
 Od. Right well. You stand in Mercia;
Where, as that aged lonely man surmised,
A monarch's head beneath a peasant's roof
Contented shelters. (*Shout.*) Hark! the cry of onset!
From thence it comes! Guard you the spoil! The rest,
That choose it, follow me!
  [*Exeunt Oddune and Saxons. Manent Edgar and Saxons.*

 Edg. Hie after them,
And bring me word what's passing. If the Dane,
  [*Exit Soldier.*
My life upon't again he bites the dust!
  (*Shouts.*)
Another shout! The contest's close at hand!
I hear the clashing of their weapons,—Well?

SOLDIER *re-enters.*

 Soldier. The Dane is overthrown! Our countrymen
Alone achieved the victory! He fled,
Ere full we came in sight. Some man of note
Is added to our band, for soon as met
Our mighty chief embraced him!

Enter ODDUNE, ALFRED, EGBERT, *and Party, with* ODDUNE'S *following.*

 Od. Countrymen,
Behold your king!
 Alf. Rise! rise! gallant friends.
We're brothers struggling in one common cause,
And by heaven's high appointment haply met!
 Od. Haply indeed! Thus at your feet I lay
The standard of the Dane!
  (*Takes the Danish standard from Edg. and lays it at Alfred's feet.*)
 Alf. What! more success!
My faithful Earl! what chance has brought thee hither?
Whence com'st thou?
 Od. From my castle, which the Danes
Beset, commanded by the brother chiefs
Hinguar and Hubba, by whose sister's skill
Was wrought that standard, call'd their fatal Rafen,
Whose ominous device, they idly feign'd
Upon the eve of victory would flap
Its magic-woven wings. It seem'd, indeed,
As if death rode upon them, marking us
His prey: for famine plied us worse within,
Than e'en the foe without. But 'twas a friend
Severe to us for our good; despairing succour,
And all munition gone, at night we made
A sally, all resolved to cut our way
Thro' the enemy, or perish sword in hand!
The Dane was unprepared—before our march
Startled his ear, our swords were at his breast!
My liege, you may believe, the weapons which
Despair first drew were wielded now by hope;
Escape was certain; but would he escape
Whom danger woo'd with chance of victory?
We fought for it; and won it!
 Alf. Fair exploit!
 Od. Of fairer yet, the news of our success,
My liege, gives hope. Such numbers throng'd to us
Upon our march, the handful, that I thought
To greet you with, has swell'd into a host—
Brave volunteers, whose pay's the leave to serve.
My liege, your queen and son?
 Alf. Oddune, forbear!
The Dane has buried them—They sleep beneath
The ruins of thy master's castle, in
The flames of which they perished. Oddune! From
A dying follower I learn'd it! Learn'd,
That treason led the accurst assailants on!
If lips that speak for the last time speak truth,
Edric has proved a traitor! Queen and child,
Except my country, Oddune, I have none—
That, now, is Alfred's all!—His all for which
Alone he cares to live: Now, could we learn
The state and numbers of the enemy,
A blow might soon be struck—Oddune!—
 Od. My liege.
 Alf. (*To himself.*) No, that were doubtful—Oddune!
 Od. Well, my liege?
 Alf. (*To himself.*) And so were that!
 Od. My liege, you spoke just now.
 Alf. Anon, my Oddune! Make the attempt myself?
Yes! Life and empire on this cast I'll stake!
But how provide myself? There is a place
In the glen where, of its shaggy vesture scant,
Its sides stand bare, and their huge ribs expose
Of solid rock; so giddy steep withal,
That down direct from the precipitous verge
You many fathoms look.—There have I mark'd
A lonely wight at the bottom couched, with harp
Playing to the idle echoes by the hour,
Admiring how they mock'd him—I will use
That harp!—will use it to expel the foe,
That thrust its master from the shining hall
To the dim cavern-cell; spill'd his heap'd dish—
O'erturn'd his cup, from all sides running o'er,
And cast him, with that golden song of his,
To roots and water,—Edwy, speak with me!
Wilt be awhile companion to thy king,
Tho' to share danger with him?
 Edwy. To share death.
 Alf. Your hand! My friends, our country must be free!
My trusty Oddune, wonder not, altho'
You've found your king to lose him for a time.
This list of trusty chiefs, with whom, through means
I need not name to thee, I have kept up
Intelligence, will show thee whom to warn
Of thy success. Summon them to repair
To Selwood Forest, there to meet their king.
There shall we meet again, my gallant friends!
Your hands, my chiefs! Soldiers, our hearts embrace!
Farewell! Be strong in hope! The land's not lost
That's left a son resolved to do her right;
And here are troops of sons, and loyal ones!
Confirm the stirring spirit of the time;
'Till it o'erspread the realm; the which throughout

With swiftest expedition bear the call
That to her rescue rouses those that love her!
Strong in her children should her mother be!
Shall ours be helpless that has sons like us?
God save our native land, whoever pays
The ransom that redeems her!—tho' the king!
There king and subject side by side shall stand!
Stand by your king, your king will stand by you!
[*Exeunt Alfred and Edwy, Oddune, and the others severally.*

END OF THE SECOND ACT.

ACT III.

SCENE I.—*The inside of Guthrum's tent.*

Enter GUTHRUM and EDRIC. 2. E. R. H.

Guth. I swear a royal booty!. Thou hast done
Great service to the Dane. With these supplies
No need to forage. Here we'll sit at ease,
And rest us from the war.
Edr. No rest for me!
Far richer holds than those which I surprised
And plunder'd, at my master's feet shall lay
Their treasure and munition
Guth. At thy friend's!
Call me not master! Call me father! Think
To thy first expedition what we owe!—
The capture of the royal Saxon's son,
The heir of Alfred.
Edr. Would his queen, as well,
Were now within thy power—But she escap'd,
Or perish'd in the flames.
Guth. Come, Edric!—speak;
What shall I give thee to reward the love,
That so hath labour'd to enrich me? Come,
Ask what thou wilt, by Odin it is thine.
Edr. Thou bad'st me call thee father. With the leave
Give me the right to hail thee by that title:
I ask thy daughter's hand.
Guth. I give it thee.
Seek her, and bring her hither.
Edr. For that boon
Command my blood! Ay, every drop of it.
[*Exit.*

Enter OSCAR, L. R. H.

Oscar. My lord, a Saxon minstrel is without:
The string he touches with a master's hand;
And as he plays, a youth, that waits upon him,
Sings to his harp rare tales of love and war,
As ever ear did list to.
Guth. Bring him in.

(*Exit Oscar, and returns with Alfred, followed by Edwy. Guthrum, who had sat down, struck by the deportment of Alfred, rises.*)

Guth. Ha! who art thou? What art thou?
Alf. I 'm the bard!
The son of fantasy!
Whose world's o' the air—to mortal vision else
Impalpable—a paragon to this—
Where he communes with forms, whose radiancy
Outshines the lustre of earth's fairest things;
Whose title, from above, earth can't confer
Or take away! Whose smile is coveted
By beauty—valour—their bright mirror, where

They see themselves more bright! Whose tributaries
Are kings themselves! Their gorgeous state but serves
To swell his strain, that doth emblazon them
Beyond their deeds or titles.
Guth. Well replied;
I like thy answer better that 'tis bold.
Sit down, sit down.—A sample of your skill.—
Thou spok'st of beauty now,—what canst thou say
In praise of it?
Alf. (*To himself.*) Thanks to the tender hand
That guided me to con the minstrel's lore,
And treasure't in my heart!
Guth. Let's taste thy skill,

ALFRED.

Would'st thou know what beauty is?
 Beauty is the queen of sighs!
Not a heart but owneth this,
 Proud or humble, light or wise.
Crowned goblets some desire;
 Some to see the banquet spread;
Some prize shining gold; and higher
 Value some the shining deed;
Safety's deem'd a gem by some;
 Danger some a jewel call;
Some to power desire to come;
 But Beauty is the prized of all!
Well the Bard her praise may sing—
 Of his soul-entrancing lyre,
She commands the master string,
 That which lends it all its fire!
Wanting which he could not sing—
 Rhymeless, numberless might be,
Nor e'er had won a name for deathless minstrelsy.

Guth. Right well thou prov'st thy title to thy name.
What does the youth that waits upon thee?
Alf. Sing
The while I play.
Guth. We'll hear him at the banquet.
(*Rises.*)
To me, thrice precious is the ruby drop
When the enchanting strain has breath'd upon it.
Thou art not old—and yet thou look'st not young;
Thy brow with wisdom graver than with years—
I'd talk with you; for great, unless I err,
Your skill in lore, we little care to search
Whose school's the battle field. Attend me!
Come.
[*Exeunt,* 1.E.L.H.

SCENE II.—*A sequestered rural spot near the camp.*

Enter INA, R.H (*leading* ETHELRED), EDITH, *and Boy.*

Edith. Your little charge is a fair healthful plant,
Whose thriving looks bespeak your careful tending.
How strong is infancy in its helplessness!
Of all that dwelt within the hold where he
Was found, no soul, they say, was spar'd but him,
Howe'er they pray'd for mercy!
Ina. Little praise
To him that sav'd him! Edric's treacherous heart
Can own no touch of mercy! Know you not
The boy is Alfred's son? His hold it was,

Which Edric with my father's host beset,
When found the chief this boy. Go on before,
We'll follow you; and mind you spare no pains
To humour him.
    [*To Boy, who exits with Eth.*, 1.E.L.H.
I should not love thee, boy;
Thy race is Ina's bane!
  Edith. Why say'st thou so?
The Saxon loves thee, Ina.
  Ina. Loves me?
  Edith. Yes!
What though his passion is not on his tongue?
His heart is full of it. It speaks in sighs—
Love's proper words. "Ne'er plainer spoke, to
    ear."
  Ina. Nay, tell me not. His heart is stone to me!
He sighs! but 'tis for freedom!
  Edith. 'Tis for you!
How love is blind to what it pines to see!
"You think him stone; belike so thinks he you.
"Look at thyself, at once thou see'st him!
"Your eyes at parting, that strain after him,
"At meeting, feast on any other thing;
"Your tongue that, when he hears not, rings with
    him
"In his hearing's noteless, as it ne'er knew sound.
"For too strong love, his love's accounted none."
  Ina. I tell thee no! His thoughts abide not *here*.
They're with his *countrymen*, some daughter fair
Of whom he loves—not Ina. Be it so.
The cheek I love shall smile, tho' not on me;
The bird I'd keep with me I will let go,
" 'Plaining the bondage that would kill with
    doating."
He's free—my father gave him liberty.
  Edith. And what for thee?
  Ina. To die, like a poor flower
That lives with only gazing on the sun;
But from her radiant lord too long shut out
By the cold cloud, in silence hangs her head,
And dies a smiling death!
  Edith. He comes.
                [*Exit*, R. H.

  Ina. Alas!
For the last time.

OSWITH *enters, perceiving* Ina. 2. E. R. H., *walks
    down* L. H.

  Os. Still, still my treacherous steps
Betray me, leading me to what I'd shun;
Yet what is ever present to my thought
Why fear my eye to see? "My thraldom's full
"If 'tis enchantment, better to enjoy
"The fatal sweetness of the powerful spell
"I strive in vain to break!"
  Ina. Saxon, thou'rt free.
  Os. Recall thy words!
  Ina. I speak my father's will.
  Os. Why does he give me liberty?
  Ina. Because
His Ina begg'd the boon.
  "*Os*. Why did she so?
"Would she had begg'd my death! I did not ask
"For freedom;—thraldom was more kind to me,
"Which chain'd me unto that I ought to fly,
"But fain would cling to. Honour did not swerve
"That was constrain'd to look upon its bane; I
"And if it look'd till it forgot itself,
"'Twas its mischance—not crime!—Now, if it
    falls,
"It falls of its own will! O maid, too fair!

ALFRED THE GREAT. 13

"Help me to 'scape the ruin thou hast wrought!
"Think—think—'tis an apostate kneels to thee!
"Instruct thy melting eye to flash with scorn—
"Teach thy sweet tongue harsh indignation's
    note—
"Erect thy form with dread severity—
"Till, like a seraph, sterner in thy frown
"For what thou look'st and breath'st of beauteous
    heaven,
"Thou aw'st me into virtue.
  Ina. Would'st thou be free,
Thou art so.
  Os. Am I? Lady, there are bonds,
The wearing which endears them to the slave,
So that he hugs them—would not be set free!
Free me from these!
  Ina. What bonds?
  Os. E'en such, as not
Our limbs imprison, but the things that rule
    them—
Our thoughts and wills—as coil about our hearts,
And keep their hold, when links of steel were wax.
  Ina. Methinks I have a guess what bonds you
    mean:
Are they not *heavy* ones when worn *alone*,
But *light* when others *share* them? Is it so?
Had'st thou such partnership would'st thou be
    free?
I would not, so had I!
  Os. It cannot be!
Half she reveals her heart, and veils her eyes.
Do her veil'd eyes unveil the other half?
Am I so bless'd, so curs'd, as to be lov'd?
"Nay, then, 1'tis fate I'd cope with, and must
    yield!"
Oh, to have fallen in battle!—to have fallen
When honour was my mistress!—to have fallen
When in her radiant eye I drew my sword,
And deem'd my life a stake not worth a thought
To venture for her smile! When wooing her,
I strode more blithely through the battlefield,
Than e'er I bounded down the festive hall!
  Ina. What makes thee wish for death?
  Os. The dread to lose
What was my more than life; but now seems
    poor—
Like to be cast away, since I have found
A good I covet more than life and it!
  Ina. What do'st thou covet so?
  Os. Thee lady, thee!
Thou art that good of value paramount!
Oh, to have met thee with a heart at large!
No solemn debt—no knotted tie upon it!
Free to be all thy own—to render thee
Its whole of love, hope, honour, loyalty—
One large, unbroken, everlasting gift—
The hand which now, in doubtful joy, I take—

Enter EDRIC, 2 E., R. H., *walks down* L. H.

How had I caught, in tranced ecstacy,
And kneeling, laid the offering at thy feet!
  Edr. Let go that hand! 'Tis mine!
  Os. What fire is this,
That with the light'ning's speed darts thro' me,
     of and feels
As all consuming!—Thine!
  Ina. Believe him not.
Oswith, believe him not—believe the maid
With thought of thee, that all forgets herself—
Casts off the bashful 'tire of virginhood,
And, unenforced, stands confest thine own!

"The eyes turn on thee, she would still avert,
"And lets thee see them, tho' they stream with
  love—
"Calls on thee with the tongue that ne'er till now
"Betray'd her secret, to receive't for thine!
"Believe him not, he sports with thee—thy heart
"Is not more surely seated in thy breast,
"Than is thy image lodg'd within my heart—
"Not more the spring of life to thee, than that
"Is life itself to Ina!" 'Fore the world
Do I proclaim me *thine*, and cleave to thee!
But plight me faith for faith.
  Os. I do, sweet maid!
  Edr. (*Drawing his sword*). My right's a bar, which
    thou must first remove!
  "*Os.* 'Twixt me and life! Strong love hath made
    me weak
"As a poor straw upon a torrent's breast,
"And bear as 'swift away!" Thy right! What
  right? (*Half drawing his sword*).
  Ina. Give me thy hand! Give me thy hand, I
    say!
Take it from thy sword! Thou'rt mine! Thy
  hand—thy arm—
Thy all! Have I not given my all for thee?
"Paid down for thee a virgin's heart, that ne'er
"Before in love was barter'd. Give me thy hand!
"Or thou'rt the falsest, most forsworn of men.
"Breaking the vow that scarce hath left thy lips,
"And I'm the poorest, most abused of maids!
Give me thy hand! Nay, an thou wilt not, thus,
Upon thy arm I'll hang, and be thy shield,
Taking the blows upon my fearless breast,
That threaten wound to thine.
  Os. (*Taking his hand from his sword.*) Thy
    right! What right?
  Edr. Dost wish to learn? Such as the bride-
    groom claims—
"As makes the lover bless his stars, and gives
"Fulfilment of his long-enduring hopes—
"As turns his blissful dreams to substances,
"So rich, past credence, still he thinks he dreams—
"Asks if he wakes—believes it—doubts it—sickens
"Lest day prove night, and laughing morning come,
"And in his very arms his treasure fade!"
  Os. (*Half drawing his sword.*) A bridegroom's
    right
  Ina. That right is thine alone!
Oh, how thy frame with fearful passion shakes!
While thy full orbs strain on thy countryman,
With deadly purpose fixed! Turn them on me!
Read who is Ina's bridegroom in her *face*!
See whom her eyes with fondness strain upon,
As thine on him with hate! " Oh what a fee
"Thou mak'st me pay for that which costs thee
  nought!"
I call thee lord—If that contents thee not,
Why then the dearer name of *husband* take,
And give me in exchange, an only look!
  Os. (*To Edr.*) Explain thy words.
  Edr. The service I have done
The Dane, he bids me name requital for;
And by his God he binds himself, whate'er
The boon, to grant it. Ina was the boon!
    (*Oswith draws his sword*.)
  Ina. List to me Oswith—Oswith—by thy love!—
My father's oath has made me his! Hear mine!
By Odin, I'll be bride to none but thee!
  Edr. Force will exact what frowardness denies!
  Os. And thou could'st wed the bride that loath'd
    thee?
  Edr. Yes.

  Os. Put up thy sword. I'd whisper thee.
        (*They whisper.*)
  Ina. Say it out.
Thy breath is mine! More than her own it feeds
Thy Ina's life! "Oh, 'tis a treacherous breath,
"To play the traitor to its mistress thus!"
Speak out I say! "Thou heed'st me not! False
  friend!
"Friend cruel and unfair, that gives me nought,
"Whilst I give all to him!"
  Edr. 'Tis well.
          [*Exit*, L. H.
  Ina. 'Tis ill!
Not half so plain thy gleaming brandish'd sword
Could threaten death, as does thy flashing eye!
  Os. Ina, thy fears are causeless. Prithee hence,
Back to the camp; whilst I revolve the means
Shall bring the course of our now thwarted loves
To prosperous issue.
  "*Ina.* I'll revolve them with thee;
"And thou shalt find how thrifty woman's wit,
"When set to work by love.
"*Os.* My Ina!—Love!
"Bride!—Wife!—for wedded they whom love has
  wed—
"I'd be alone."
  Ina. I will not leave thee! Come!
We'll go to the camp together.
  Os. Sweet, my way
Lies this way.
  Ina. So does mine, then.
  Os. Nay, farewell!
  Ina. You leave me not! I'll cling to thee till
    death
Disjoins us! Drag me if thou wilt, I'll ne'er
Let go my hold! Oh was there ever maid
So lost for love! that knelt—that bent the knee—
Pleaded her cause with her bold tongue—"paid
  tribute,
"Large as her eyes could furnish, of her tears"
To an unheeding lover, deaf to her,
And scarce confest an hour!

  Re-enter EDRIC, 1. E. L. H.

  Edr. Was it for this
Thou sent'st me hence? to give thee pause for
  dalliance!
Traitor!
  Os. Ha!
  Edr. Coward!
        (*Both draw.*)

  Enter GUTHRUM *and* ALFRED, U. E. L. H.

  Guth. Hold! forbear! Who stirs
There's but a single step 'twixt him and death,
And he has trod it. What's your cause of
  quarrel?
Ina, my child! what share hast thou in't?
  What!
Dost turn from me?
                (*Angrily.*)
  Ina. My father!
                (*Crossing to him.*)
  Guth. There! there! there!
                (*Pressing her to him.*)
Did I speak roughly to thee! Silly fawn,
To start at but a sound! Art thou in tears?
It does concern thee, then? How, Ina, speak!
Dost hear me? Answer, girl! Well; never
  heed.

You would if you could! No matter! Noble
    Edric
Declare thy cause of quarrel to thy friend.
  Ina. Thou'rt not his friend!! Call not thyself
    his friend!
  Guth. My Ina, but I must! and so must
    thou——
  Ina. Never!
  Guth. What's that! My child, beware! You
    know
I brook not thwarting! must not be gainsaid!
Call him thy friend! Come! Show me thou'rt my
    child!
My flesh! my blood! that owe themselves to me,
And should be subject to me! Will't thou
    speak?
Take counsel! Something's rising in my heart
That bodes not good to thee! Once more I say,
Resist me not! Submit! Call him thy friend.
Art silent still? Now minstrel, prove thou'rt
    wise!
I found thee so when we discours'd of peace!
Of war!—the duties subjects owe to kings,
And kings to subjects. Now propound the means
Behoves a father take, who would untie
A wilful daughter's tongue!
  Alf. Force but subdues
The weak; still, with the strong, 'tis met by
    force.
Was never found the noble nature yet
That crouch'd e e a frown! 'Tis sway'd with
    smiles for
Chiding her nature thou chid'st thy own!
She's thy soul's bright and fair reflecting glass!
But look at her! "Sits not thy upper lip,
"All manly as it is, and bold, to her's,
"More proudly firm upon thy nether one,
"Than her's upon its fellow!" Vauntest thou,
As only late thou didst, rebuke with thee,
Given as rebuke, ne'er mended railing yet?
Then is thy boast her pardon! Give me favour
For speaking thus my thought.
  Guth. Thou dost my wish.
I like thy frankness! Yes; I see! You're
    right!
She's all her father's child! Come to me Ina!
    (*She rushes into his arms.*)
What would'st thou do for me?
  Ina. Aught that I could.
  Guth. Ah, there my Ina speaks! I like thee
    thus!
Thus, Ina, when thou hang'st upon my neck,
And gazest in my face! My Ina, list;
I'll tell thee wherefore I'd entreat thee call
The Saxon friend. I've sworn to give thee to
    him.
  "*Ina.* Without my heart! What, father, give
    my hand
"Without my heart? Not so would'st thou give
    thine,
"And make a league of friendship with thy
    hand.
"Thy heart protested 'gainst! And what were
    that,
"Gompar'd to one of love? A league of friend-
    ship.
"That bar'd a friend out, and enclosed a foe!
"Would'st thou do that? Thou would'st not give
    a smile
"Without thy soul's consent. And would'st thou
    have
"Thy Ina give her hand without her heart?"

  Guth. Dread Odin has my oath!
  Ina. So has he mine!
  Guth. What hast thou sworn?
  Ina. Eternal truth to love!
  Guth. Thou dost not know the passion? But
    thou dost!
'Tis clear! I see too sure thou art love's thrall!
Upon thy cheek his crimson pennon waves!
Thy down-cast eyes pay homage to his sway!
Thy heaving breast by its commotion shows
The conqueror is within! I see his power
Confessed in every fibre of thy frame!
Whom dost thou love? Who has lit up this
    flame?
  Ina. (*Kneeling.*) Thou, father, thou; whose
    fondness for thy child
Would sketch for her the man thou'dst have her
    wed.
How he should be among his peers in rank.
And that the first—without a peer in worth.
Most brave—most true—most generous—most
    good.
"Fit to be challenger of all the field,
"In all achievements of supreme renown,
"And bear the palm from all!" Nor yet to lack
Those qualities of visage, and of f$_o$rm,
Which to these other richer graces join'd
Make the consummate man. But that I saw
My father such a man, I should have deem'd
A phantom 'twas he drew for me; for ne'er
Except in him, saw I embodied wealth
Of so rare worth—until I saw it there!
  Guth. What's this to me?
  Ina. The being of thy child—
Thy Ina—thy dear Ina—who forgets
Her father 'tis she's kneeling to, as tho'
He were a stranger to her; but now leaps
Into his bosom! Oh, I'd like to see
The harm could reach me here!
  Guth. The Saxon dies!
  Ina. No, no!
  Guth. He spurn'd the proffer of his life,
When forfeit to the God!
  Ina. Nay, hear me!
  Guth. Spurn'd
My friendship! Guthrum's friendship!
  Ina. No!
  Guth. He did!
I lov'd him, tho' my foe, because I mark'd
His prowess in the fight! "I could have thought
"The God himself had turn'd against his sons,
"And, angry, sided with their enemies!"
He was my captive! He had bled to Odin!
I proffer'd him my friendship, would he make
Alliance with the Dane, to snatch him from
The altar; and he spurned me! Ay, refused
The hand of a victorious king, thro' faith
To an uncrowned fugitive! He did!
I spared him at my child's beseeching! He
That spurn'd the parent now would win the
    child!
He dies!
  Alf. (*Aside to Guthrum.*) Thy Ina dies! See how
    she hangs,
Half-dead, already on thy shoulder! Much
Thou lov'st her! If none other calls thee father,
Beware thou art not childless!
  Guth. Am I in the wrong?
Demand I more than is a father's due?
What is her life but portion of my breath?
  Alf. A portion thou would'st give thy breath
    to save?

Guth. Thou sayest right.
Alf. A portion, too, which she
Would render up, not only to save thine,
But let thee breathe with ease.
Guth. Thou sayest right;
Yet bows she not her fancy to my will.
Alf. She cannot.
Guth. How?
Alf. You ask; and you have lov'd!
Guth...How know you that?
Alf. Who has not felt the flame?
Your passion was repaid.
Guth. How know you that?
Alf. How know I that? From naught but mutual love
A flower, consummate rich like that, could grow!
Where fairest things that harmonise unite!
E'en such a skin should such a mould ensheath,
To such a heart, be casket such a mould;
Such lineaments compose the beauteous face,
Of such a neck that makes its graceful seat;
And such a mould, and heart, and face be served
By such a minstrel as that tuneful tongue.
This speaks the mingling of accordant hearts,
Throbbing in fervent unity; that one
No thought, no wish, no hope, no joy can lodge,
But finds its fellow at the other's core!
Guth. Minstrel thou'rt right! Deep does thy wisdom search;
Her mother, Eva, was my only love,
As I was her's! Tho' daughter of my foe.
She left her father, friends, land, faith, and all
To follow me. She did!—She did!
Alf. And that's
Her child, in whom the passion that bless'd thee,
Thou'dst turn into a curse.
Guth. I like not that!
Thou mak'st too bold to say I'd curse my child!
Alf. Look at her!
Guth. Thou art right! (*Raises her up and embraces her.*) Say on! Say on!
Yet where's the profit? Win me Odin's ear,
And move the God to give me back my oath!
Thou but perplexest me! Since thou'rt so wise,
Show me the way not to forswear myself;
And yet not keep my oath.
Alf. Two oaths the God
Has register'd; one only can be kept.
Which he accepts, the God himself decide.
You say he rules the sword; then to the sword
Entrust the cause, and these the terms of strife.
Who masters first his adversary's sword
And yet not sheds his blood, be his the maid!
Os. Content!
Edr. Content!
Ina. Oswith, this chain's of gold,
(*Still leaning on her father.*)
That never knew alloy—cunningly wrought—
An amulet, that ever faithful guards
The wearer's wishes; proves it false to thine,
Drop it into the grave where I shall lie,
Ere by its treachery thy rival thrives.
Guth. And Edric, thou receive this ring from me.
The hand that wears it, holds its weapon true,
If faithful to the Dane, as thou to me.
(*Goes up with Ina,* C.)
Alf. I have a ring, a charmed bauble too.
Power to the hand it graces, does it give
O'er falsehood to prevail. 'Tis his who'll take it—
But who would wear it, and its virtue prove,
Must first affirm he owns a loyal heart—
True to the king that first his homage claim'd,
The land that gave him birth—Wilt take it, thou?
Edr. The ring I'll trust is this I now put on,
The guard of my good sword!
(*Goes up* L. H.)
Alf. Wilt take it, thou?
Os. Tho' to the king I'm true
That first my homage claim'd—true to the land
That gave me birth; yet more, than true to those,
The thrall of love, I dare not take the ring.
Alf. Show me thy hand—my countryman—'tis on!
'Tis a true hand—for ne'er would fit the ring,
Disloyal finger yet. Look at it well!
Lo! speak I not the truth?
Os. (*Recognising Alf.*) My liege!
Alf. Beware!
In whose but a true subject's hands would place
A king his life. Be of good heart! No doubt,
Palsy thy arm! The wishes of thy love,
Thy king, are with thee! Heaven be with thee too!
(*Crosses* R.H.)
Guth. Away!, I'll follow you; and see, myself,
This bloodless trial made.
[*Exeunt Oswith and Edric,* L.H
Here, minstrel, take
My child! Support her! Cheer her to abide
The issue of their strife.
[*Exit* L. H.
Alf. (*Supporting Ina.*) Fair maiden, take
The minstrel's word, thy lover wins the game!
Thy fears are wrongs, where wrong thou least would'st do!
Doubt on thy champion did another cast
How would disdain arouse thy languid lip;
Colour thy frozen cheek from snow to flame;
And the expired lustre of thine eye
Re-kindle with its lightning! Maiden, list!
The hand's best sinew ever is the heart!
Thy lover's is the sound one! Think of that!
That's right! Look up! Take courage! Oswith throws
His brand away, and grapples Edric's! Ha!
Keep thy hold, Edric, if thou can'st! A child's—
An infant's—is it to thy rival's grasp!
Look on thy lover, maiden! His chief's eye
Upon him, double is a vassal's strength;
What then the lover's, in his mistress' eye,
That strives for victory, and she the prize?
He sees thee! Mark you, how his frame distends,
As though with superhuman vigour fraught,
At his good angel's sight! Wave, maiden fair,
Wave your white arm to him! 'Twere ten times worth
A royal pennon in a monarch's hand,
Cheering the champion of his challeng'd crown!
You, see! You see! Now puts he forth his might!
Edric gives way! He faints! His limbs are wax,
Wrestling with limbs of steel! He falls! His sword
Waves o'er his head, in noble Oswith's hand.
Hold up! Nay, gasp not! It were wrong to die,
Slain by thy gallant lover's victory!

Enter GUTHRUM, *leading* OSWITH, L. H.

Guth. There, Saxon, take my child; but thou'rt my thrall.
Thou must not bear her hence.
Alf. He should not! Guthrum!

Where'er I speak of thee I'll give thee out
Indeed a royal chief! Farewell!
(Going R. H.)
Guth. Not yet.
By Odin thou shalt join our feast! I say
Thou shalt not go! I like thy company!
I'd hear thy harp again! Come! Follow all.
[*Exeunt* U. E. L. H.

" *Re-enter* EDRIC.
" *Edr.* Foil'd, but not yet o'ercome. The baffled foe
" That will not turn a friend, is like to prove
" A deadly one! Oswith has won the maid,
" But not possess'd her yet! I'll mar his love!
" That minstrel is not what he seems! Me he shuns—
" Communes with Oswith freely—Oswith knows him!
" Someone of note—a prize to Guthrum—which
" If Oswith lets escape, he wrongs the Dane;
" And thence I'll work his ruin! To the banquet!
" I'll watch their every movement; and unmask him,
" Tho' I should tear the visor from his face."
[*Exit.*

END OF THE THIRD ACT.

ACT IV.

SCENE .I.—*The inside of Guthrum's Tent.*—*Discovered seated* Guthrum, Oswith, Ina, *Chiefs,* Alfred, Edwy, *&c., &c.*

Enter EDRIC, *through centre.*

Guth. Come Edric, tho' not Fortune's friend, thou'rt mine.
Why didst thou stay behind? Sit by me, Edric.
Look to the minstrel—see that his goblet's full—
Let it o'erflow—see to't!
Os. You feast not, love.
Ina. No more do you.
Os. I do not care to feast.
When the heart banquets, viands are pass'd by!
Edith (*Entering,* c.) Your little Saxon favourite wants you, Ina,
He clamours for you, nought can quiet him.
Ina. Nay, try and soothe him. If he baffles thee,
Why bring him hither, then!
[*Exit Edith,* c.
Guth. Come, strike your harp!
We'd hear a strain; and prithee let it be
A warlike one. "The triumph of the Dane—
" Can'st thou play that?
" *Alf.* Accursed be the bard
" That sings his country's shame! Her glory, chief,
" I'll sing! My harp hath often rung with it!
" Shall ring again! Or if the theme be done,
" The strings, which many a year my hands have kiss'd,
" I'll tear from their lov'd frame, tho' as they snap
" My heart-strings break, and I partake the ruin.
" *Guth.* By Odin, but thou'rt bold. I like thee for't.

" Play what thou wilt." Well, what's to be the strain?
Alf. The downfall of Cadwallon.
Guth. What was he?
Alf. The Saxons' foe.

ALFRED *plays while* EDWY *sings.*

Cry, cry to the eagle, her feast is prepar'd;
Cadwallon the Lion, his falchion has bar'd!
Ten thousand spears dance to his trumpet's song,
As his march in thunder rolls along!
Does she hear? Will she come? Is she hurrying down?
All's ready, and waiting for her alone!
But the might's with the right,
From the cloud breaks the light;
And the head high at morning—may lie low ere the night!

" But why does the Saxon, Oswald, kneel?
" Is't for his prayers he is dress'd in steel?
" And wherefore kneels his Saxon bands?
" Do they pray with their weapons in their hands?
" Or are they contented to banquet the guest
" Cadwallon the Lion has call'd to his feast?
But the might's with the right,
From the cloud breaks the light;
" And the head high at morning—may lie low ere the night!

" Not long did the Saxon kneel.—he arose
" With a shout that made leap the bold hearts of his foes;
" And on he rush'd, and down he bore
" The spears that hunted him before.
" And the trumpet that sounded the first for the field—
" Cadwallon the Lion's was the first that was still'd!
" For the might's with the right,
" From the cloud breaks the light;
" And the head high at morning—may lie low ere the night!"

But where is the eagle was called to the feast?
She is come! but Cadwallon salutes not his guest,
She has fallen to her meal without beckon or word;
She screams with her glee, but her mirth is unheard;
She has perch'd on the head of the warrior's son,
And the blood-drop that falls from her beak is his own.
For the might's with the right,
From the cloud breaks the light:
And the head high at morning may lie low ere the night

Guth. Well ne! a strain that for a warrior's ear do
" For me, thrice precious is the ruby drop
" Since the en h n ing strain has breath'd upon it!" c a t
Taste, friends. (*Officer presents goblet to Guthrum*).
Come, lips to brims; there's magic in
The cup! The health of him that pours it in—
" The bard," the king of song, whose praise to sound
Becomes and not disparages the lips
Of kings themselves!
Alf. (*Aside*). A regal nature his!
There's something in thee, Guthrum, I could claim
Close kindred with; but there's no grasping hands
For thee and me, save in the deadly strife
That ends the hope of one of us! I've gain'd
All needful knowledge. Ward of caution none
They keep—in our complete discomfiture

Secure. An easy prey they're sure to fall
To sudden onset from a band like ours,
Strong in their course and resolute of heart.

Enter ELSWITH, *pale, emaciated, and in wretched attire, through centre.*

Guth. Ha! who art thou?
Els. Who play'd that strain?
Guth. Thou ask'st
As if reply were not a boon, but debt!
Whence gottest thou that air of high command?
Els. From misery!
" Guth. She strangely teaches thee,
"Making thee stately that makes others bow!
"What seek'st thou here?"
Els. I heard a strain without;
I'd learn who play'd that strain.
Guth. That harper.
Els. He!
Hope, thou did'st right to mock me. I have found thee
Still a dissembler, and I'd trust thee still!
But now farewell, thou thing of p e i u tongue
But hollow heart! "Smooth face that's but a mask
"To cover what we loathe. Great promiser,
"Little performer! Coiner of false smiles,
"That turn out tears at last." I've done with thee!
(*She sits in the centre,* R. H.)
Otho. Thou sitt'st in Guthrum's presence.
Els. What of that?
I have sat down with Despair—a greater chief
Than Guthrum—one could make him gnash his teeth!
Ay, could he, mighty as your master is!
I've sat down with Despair! Now show me Death!
I'll take my seat by him! I fear him not!
" Alf. Contain thyself, my heart!—It is my queen!
" Guth. Her mind's distracted!
" Alf. No!—It is her heart.
" Ina. Perhaps she hungers. Give her food!
(*They present food to her.*)
" Els. Too rich!
" Famine partakes not such! She feeds on haws,
" Acorns, and roots, and berries! Give me these!
" For these we thank the Dane!
" Guth. You thank the Dane!
" Ha!
" Alf. 'Tis a woman in affliction speaks!
" Guth. And let her speak! Yet does she mar the cheer.
" Remove her
" Els. Touch me not! Stand off! My name
" Is Woe! I am the mark of Wrath! Behold
" How he has smitten me, and smitten me
" That mine own eyes don't know me! One hot day,
" Parch'd up with thirst and hunger, of a brook
" I stoop'd to drink, and saw myself, and scream'd
" At presence of a stranger. Time makes things
" Unlike the things they were, but Wrath's the changer!"
Guth. Persuade her to go hence.
Els. I hear you! Ill
You entertain the guests you force to greet you!
Guth. We force!
Els. Ay! burn them out of house and home!
Murder their husbands, and their children! Scatter

Their friends, that where a thousand troop to-day
Not one is found to-morrow!—Bid them search
For viands in the larders of the wolf
And vulture! which, deriding them, perforce
They come to you.
Guth. Hence with her! force her hence!
Alf. (*Starting up.*) Who hand of force lays on her, let him die!
And save thy manly name from the reproach,
That in thy presence, misery like this
Was offer'd insult with impunity,
And in the sacred person of a woman!
Els. The voice, too!—No! it is not, cannot be!
Guth. Heard'st what she said?
Alf. I did.
Guth. Was't true?
Alf. Free speech
Accord'st thou me?
Guth. 'Tis thine.
Alf. The truth she speaks.
But one she seems 'mongst thousands, whom thy sword,
Ravenous of conquest, hath made widows of,
And childless mothers! Who, this hour thou feast'st,
Are famishing!—in their own land, without
Abode or food—and curse the hour when first
Thou trodd'st upon their shores!
Guth. In their own land?
(*He quits his seat, and approaches Alfred,* c.)
Surely I heard thee not! In their own land?
'Tis mine! all mine! their land! air! water! They
Themselves! All mine! Mine! Mine! They!
Thou, ay thou!
That mocks't me! brav'st me! Thou, I say, art mine!
My thrall! my slave! a worm! thing for my foot
To tread upon! Confess it!
Alf. No!
Guth. Thou wilt not?
Know'st thou the man thou tempt'st? Do'st hear
" me? Think'st thou
" I speak to thee by my page, to whom thou'rt free
" To lend but half an ear? May'st pass excus'd
" To bear no duty in thine air, thine eye?
" May'st answer by a nod, or not at all?" I'm Guthrum!
He whose breath's thy life! A look—
An only look of whose incensed wrath
Might strike thee dead! Do'st thou not tremble?
Alf. No!
Guth. Up, slave, and beg thy life!
Alf. Why beg for that
I deem not worth the only asking for?
Moreover, that thou hast not power to take?
Guth. Not power to take? Was never Guthrum brav'd
By mortal man before! Not power to take!
" Guthrum is but a child! Strong as my wrath,
" My stronger wonder overpowers it quite,
" And from a tempest quells me to a calm!
" The reason? Come! I'll let thee have thy way,
" Giv'st thou me but the reason. Come, the reason?
" Be it but half-sufficient, it shall weigh
" Acquittance of thee. Come, the reason—come!"
Alf. Your royal word is warrant for my safety.
What by your leave I speak, yourself forbids you
To turn to evil 'gainst me.

ALFRED THE GREAT. 19

Guth. Right, by Odin!
You're always right! and you may speak again,
And freely as before. (*Resumes his seat,* L. H.)
  Ina. I prithee, Oswith,
Persuade thy countryman to leave the tent.
What now is safety may anon prove danger,
Fierce as 'tis sudden is my father's wrath;
And ever in the hour of social cheer
Most to be fear'd and look'd for—speak to him!
Conjure him to go hence. (*Oswith crosses to* L. H.)
  Os. Had he a steed——
  Ina. A steed?—An easy thing, my Oswith!
Two—
The fleetest in the camp—shall be at hand,
Ready caparison'd—behind the tent—
That way conduct him hence.
  [*Whispers an Attendant, who crosses
    and exits,* R. H., *while Oswith crosses
    to Alfred,* R. H.
  Os. My liege, your ear.
  Edr. (*To Guth.*) You mark, my lord, he whispers him.
  Guth. I do; and what of that?
  Edr. They understand each other.
  Guth. Think'st thou so?
  Edr. Yes; I'll have an eye upon them.
  Guth. I heed them not.

  Enter EDITH *and* ETHELRED, C. L. H.

  Els. Whose child is that? not thine!
  Edith He is not mine.
  Els. He's not a Danish child.
  Edith. He's not.
  Els. Is he a Saxon, then? Is he a Saxon, then?
  Edith. He is a Saxon child.
  Els. A Saxon! Pray you, let me see his face!
He's mine!
  Edith. He shrin   from thee. He knows thee
    not.   ks
  Els. Me can he know, that do not know myself?
He'll know my voice! My child! My Ethelred!
He knows it not! and is my voice changed too?
Or does my face false witness bear so strong,
He gives not credence to his mother's voice!
He is my child! Believe it for my tears,
My choking utterance, my bended knees,
And my imploring arms that sue to you,
And ask you for my child!
  Alf. (*Aside.*) Does Providence
Vouchsafe such mercy!
  Guth. If the child is thine,
Thou'lt know where it was found.
  Els. Too well I know!
Both when and where! A castle did ye sack,
Whose tenant was the mother of that child.
At night the cry arose, "*The Dane!*" "*The Dane!*"
And then the bursting gate—the clash of arms!
"The shout—the yell—the shriek—the groan—
      which rage,
"And cruelty, and fear, and pain supply,
"To make the concert fell of savage war!"
That mother's care too safe had lodg'd her child
In the remotest chamber of the whole.
She ask'd for it, "*The Dane!*" was the reply.
She would have sought it; but they held her back,
And cried, "*The Dane!*" he shrieked to be set
      free!
"Now threaten'd! now implor'd! but all in vain!
"'*The Dane!*' was all the answer she could get!"
They forc'd her thence in cruel duty! Ay!
In duty forc'd the mother from her child;
While lent the Dane a torch to light her path,
Her flaming towers that blaz'd about her boy!
And she went mad! yet still they bore her on;
No other heed to her distraction gave,
Except to cry, "*The Dane! The Dane! The Dane!*"
    (*Sinks exhausted upon a seat, clasping
      her forehead. Guth. and Edr. whisper.*)
  Els. Alas; they give not credence to my words!
Will no one plead for me? My countryman,
      (*Crossing to Alf.*)
Essay your art! Hast not some melting strain—
Such as draw tears whether they will or not?
As moves. (*Recognising Alf.*) I've found him!
  Edr. (*Coming forward.*) Whom? Whom hast
      thou found?
  Els. (*Recollecting herself.*) My boy!
  Edr. (*Aside.*) I thought she meant the minstrel.
  Alf. Yes!
She knows me, and I am a husband still!
I am a father, and a husband still!
"Oh, happiness, thou comest out of time!
"Thou choosest ill the place to greet me in!
"Thou mockest me to hold thine arms to me!
"I dare not rush to their embrace! I'm poor,
"With all the wealth thou say'st is mine again!
"I dare not touch it! Better were it far,
"I had not now been told on't."
  Guth. Take the boy!
But first true answer to our question give.
The castle where we found him was the king's!
Clad as no vassal's offspring was the child.
If thou his mother art, thou art the queen!
      (*Crossing centre.*)
Art thou so?
  Alf. (*Rising.*) Guthrum, to the test I put
Thy nature! If 'tis worthy of thy state,
Thy prosperous fortune, and thy high renown,
Approve it now. Lo, Guthrum, do I play
The traitor for thy honour! In thy power
Thou hold'st the son and consort of thy foe!
Of Alfred! Use thy fortune as beseems thee!
Swear by thy God, they shall receive from thee
Safeguard of life and honour.
  Guth. Ay, by Odin.
  Els. Would'st thou not take a ransom for us?
  Guth. Yes!
  Els. What ransom wilt thou take?
  Guth. Thy husband's crown!
  Els. Alas! he will not ransom us with that!
  Alf. He should not!
  Guth. Why?
  Alf. He wears it for his people.
The day he put it on he vow'd himself
Of them the father! To their parent land
It wedded him! His proper consort she!
'Twixt him and them, he knows not wife or
      child,
He dares allow to stand!
  Guth. Minstrel, thou rav'st!
He has not nature, who 'gainst nature's law
Could so deny his heart!
  Alf. He may have more!
  Guth. What?
  Alf. The command of her. The attribute
Of kings who feel the import of their titles.
Which stops their ears against her piercing cries!
Which shuts their eyes against her thrilling looks!
Which lifts them so 'bove earth, they seem as tho'
They sat in some attendant, brighter sphere,'
Wherefrom they look'd and rul'd her!
  Guth. Well thou said'st
Thy world was of the air! Thou do'st not speak

Of things of earth! Thy sayings are not sooth!
I would thy king were here to prove thee but
A dreamer! With those jewels in his eye,
He would not see his crown! Yea, tho' it shone
Bright as it did before I thiun'd its studs!
Could'st find thy king?
   Alf. I could.
   Guth. Go seek him, then.
And whent   u find'st him, greet him from me
                   ltho—
"*Thy queen and son are now in Guthrum's power,*
Pay thou but homage to the Dane, they're free."
   Alf. I take my leave.
   Els. Guthrum. A boon!
   Guth. What is't?
   Els. I'd send a message to my lord!
   Guth. Thou shalt.
Stand you apart, that freely they confer.
                  (*All retire up.*)
   Els. And do'st thou go; and wilt thou leave us
      here?
   Alf. I must. Alas! thou know'st not what thou
      say'st!
   Els. Thou'lt leave us here! Do'st thou not love
      our child?
   Alf. Beyond my life!
   Els. And me?
   Alf. Beyond our child!
   Els. And must thou leave me? "Oh! I have
      searched for thee
"Many, and many a day! Now fear'd thee dead!
"Now hop'd thee living! Search'd for thee alone!
"One falling now; and now another off;
"With my strong love unequal to keep pace.
"Sleeping in woods and caves! On foot by dawn,
"Ne'er giving o'er t'll night again! Now food,
"Now nothing! Scantily I far'd to-day;
"Yet 'twas not hunger brought me here, but thou,
"In desperate hope to find thee! Art thou found,
"But to be lost again?"
   Alf. "So were I found,
"Went I not instant hence" Look in my eyes,
And read the husband and the father there,
In nature's undissembling language vouch'd!
But, hear the king!
   Els. Well!
   Alf. Paramount of all,
My public function! Husband—father—friend—
All titles, and all ties are merged in that!
Approve thyself the consort of a king!
I leave thee to return to thee. Return,
With freedom for thy chi'd—for thee—myself—
For all—for all must perish, or be free!
And soon I come! So cheer thy heart with hope!
Farewell!
   Els. (*Aloud.*) You'll bear my duty to my lord.
   Alf. I will.
   Els. Your hand that you will keep your word.
   Alf. There, lady.
   Els. "Be thy hand my missive! Thus—
"Thus with my tears I write my errand on't—
"And with my lips—a faithful signet, seal it!"
O, countryman! perhaps nor he nor thou
Shalt ever see more! I feel as one
Amerc'd of life—that shakes a hand with all—
And asks a blessing from the meanest tongue!
Thy blessing, minstrel, ere thy mistress dies.
   Alf. What love would ask to light on head be-
      lov'd—
What faith and virtue Heaven's own warrant have
To ask of Heaven—light on thy honoured head!
   Edr. I'll see him eye to eye, ere he departs.

   Alf. Farewell!
   Edr. Stay, minstrel. Let me see thy face!
               (*Edric stops Alfred forcibly.*)
   Os. All's lost! (*Half drawing his sword.*)
   Alf. (*Turning fully and sternly upon Edric.*)
      There, traitor!
      (*Edric, utterly confounded, staggers back.*)
   Os. Fly my liege! Away.
      [*Exeunt Alfred, Edwy, and Oswith,* 1. E. R. H.
   Guth. (c.) What moves thee, Edric? What's the
      matter? Speak!
Why is thine eye-ball fixed, thy mouth agape?
What ails thy blood, that it forsakes thy check?
Why shakes thy frame?
   Edr. My liege!
   Guth. Out with it!
   Edr. The minstrel!
   Guth. What of the minstrel?
   Edr. Oswith plays thee false!
No minstrel leaves the camp; but Oswith thence,
Treacherous to thee, conducts thine enemy,
Alfred, the Saxon King;
   Guth. Ha! Follow them.
Stop his retreat! Away! Alive or dead,
Have them before us!
            [*Exeunt Edric, Otho, and others.*
   Els. Mercy! Guthrum! Mercy!
                (*Clashing of swords.*)
   Guth. Remove her!
   Els. "Where's the lightning! What! no bolt
"To blast the impious hand that threatens death,
"To his anointed head." O mercy mercy!
      [*She is forced off, Edith following with*
      the child.
   Edr. (*Without,* R.) Traitor, give way.
   Os. (*Without,* R.) Make way—for none I'll give.
              (*The fighting continues.*)
   Guth. Who aids him? Is there treason in the
      camp?
That thus the contests lasts. Give me my sword.
   Ina. (*Kneeling to Guthrum*). My father!
   Guth. (*Not heeding her.*) Ho! my buckler and
      my spear!
"With mine own hand will I transfix him!"
   Ina. Father!

       Enter EDRIC, *wounded,* 1. E. R. H.

   Edr. At last, my lord, we've o'erpowered him.
   Guth. Whom?
   Edr. Oswith.
   Guth. And Alfred?
   Edr. He has escaped, I fear!
   Guth. Lay Oswith in chains.
   Ina. My father!
   Guth. To the god
I give him! Odin, take him! He is thine!
By thy victorious spear he bleeds to thee.
                    [*Exit Edr.,* R. H.
Give him my child, the traitor! Give him my
      blood!
I'd pour it out upon the altar first!
I would with mine own hand! I'd look on her!
And do it! Look on her! Up girl and hence!
Ha! do I see a statue, or my child?
"That check is marble by its hue! Those eyes
"The chisel makes as good, for any touch
"Of sense that's in them!" What is it I've
      done?
"Oh! they have lov'd and pin'd, and lov'd again
"As fresh as ever." Take her to her couch!
She'll sleep—will she sleep? There, gently! I am
      grown

From fire to ice with looking on her. Ha!
For what have I done this? Stand you all here?
What! have I paid so dearly for the prize,
And do you let it go? Pursue! Pursue!
[*Exeunt*, R. H.

END OF ACT IV.

ACT V.

SCENE I.—*Ina's Tent. A recess in the centre, with a curtain drawn before it.*

Enter GUTHRUM, OSCAR, *and* EDITH,
1. E. L. H.

Guth. What say the priests?
Osc. You may not spare his life!
Your oath to Odin must be kept, unless
His country he forswears, and serves the god—
Conditions which he spurns. "Would else the tide
"Of your great nation's prosperous fortune ebb
"To an eternal drought!" Among the ranks
They run, thy oath reiterating, and, with words
Ambiguous, starting fears, you may retract,
And curse your people!
Guth. Let their altar reek!
Blood rain upon them till it drown them! Leave
The tent!
Osc. Shall they prepare to sacrifice?
Guth. Tell them, if for command of mine they wait,
I will not give it!—No! not for their god!
[*Exit Osc.*, L. H.
She speaks not?
Edith. Nay, my lord, at times a word;
But none that leads to certain inference—
Guth. Has she not slept?
Edith. Nought but unnatural sleep—
"Rest that might pass for wakefulness—that scarce
"Doth shut the lid—which weariness itself
"Beholding, ere 'twould taste, would watch; it seems
"So far from sweet." All listlessness without,
While all within is stirring!
Guth. I'll not see her.
Edith. My lord?
Guth. I did not speak; or, if I did,
'Twas not to thee! I thought myself a father!
I thought as never father lov'd his child
I lov'd my Ina! "'Twas my pride to show it;
"Yea, even when she ruled me like a child!
I us'd to think that of my fiercest mood
She was the mistress that from my wildest flight
Could call me, if my eye but lit on her,
As the lov'd lure, the falcon!—and I've kill'd her!
I'm not a father!—I did never love her
But as a child—a toy! Come, show her to me!
Undraw the curtain! He that makes a corse
Of what he loves, may sure be flint enough
To look upon't.

(*Edith undraws the curtain, and Ina is discovered sitting in a state of fixed abstraction. Edith raises her, and leads her forward to a couch, Ina moving as if it were mechanically.*)

Leave us to ourselves. [*Exit Edith* R. H.

"Why, 'tis enough to make the sickly heart
"Break out in laughter, when the very work
"Our eyes could weep them tearless at, our hands
"May boast the making of!
(*Approaches, and sits down beside her on* L. H.)
My Ina! Ina!—
My child! you'll speak to me?—What are you ill?
How feel you?—You look well!—There, my own girl,
Lie in your father's bosom!—Speak to him!
What say'st thou, sweet?—Was't not about to speak!
Thou wast. Go on—go on!—Speak to me Ina!
Or I'll go mad! Do'st hear?—On my knees,
I pray you speak to me!—Now, this is wilful!
"Away!—you but dissemble—'Tis put on!"—
For shame, for shame! You've seen my eyes in tears!
You've seen my knees upon the ground!—You know
It is your father—your old father, and
You'll not speak to him!—Think you he can't see?
Why, any one could do't! "To fix the eye
"And keep the visage motionless, and sit
"As you were riveted to your seat!" A child
Were scant of wit that lack'd such obvious power—
Of 'simulation! I renounce you, Ina! (*Going.*)
Will you not speak to me, my child? Speak to me!
(*Returns.*)
A word—a whisper—anything!—a sign—
To show me that you are not worse than dead—
Alive and just the same! I can be rash!
I can give way to fury!—I will try
If life be in thy heart!
(*Draws his dagger, and rushes up to her.*)
I'd scare a stone!
(*Wild discordant music is heard without, Ina starts up and clasps her hands.*)
Guth. Ha!
Ina. There 'tis
Guth. She speaks!—She is alive!
"*Ina.* I've listened for't
"So long, I fear'd 'twould never come!
"*Guth.* What, Ina? (*Music again.*)
"*Ina.* Again!
"*Guth.* They do prepare to lead him forth;
"The sacrifice will presently begin!
"They make a pretext of their god to mock
"My power!"
Ina. He's ready!—Let me go to him!
Guth. To whom? Thy lover?
Ina. I should like to get
My father's blessing first!
"*Guth.* Thou hast it, Ina!
"*Ina.* I know I have. Who says he does not love me?
"I'd not believe it, tho' he were to kill me!
"He'd do't in madness, and he'd kill himself
When he had found he had done it! Bless his Ina?
"He always blesses me—at morning when
"He sees me first, and then, again, at night;
"Yea, oft'times thro' the day! He'd bless me tho'
"I broke his heart; and I'll bless him, altho'
"He has broken mine!"
Guth. She knows me not!
Ina. We'll wed
As never lovers did. We'll have our nuptials

Of a new fashion. Who'd be bid to them
Let him bring tears with him, he's welcome—such
As gush with sobs! We'll have no smiles at
   them!
"The meanest churl gets handfuls when he weds!
"Nor songs! such minstrelsy a beggar buys
"For thanks!" No, give us shrieks and laughter!
   but
Such laughter as it withers joy to hear!
As breaketh from the heart of madness! as
Resounds from lips that wish their owners dead!
   "*Guth.* What mean those words, my child?"
   "*Ina.* I'll wed him as
"Ne'er wedded maid, to let him never from
"My side; but dwell in such entrancement with
   him,
"The day for us may go without his sun,
"And night without her cloud! All converse
   cease,
"Of tongue or eye; that not ourselves shall
   break
"The silence sweet of our deep ecstacy."
   Guth. Perception's all within; without is none.
Passion hath drunk up sense! I feel a touch
Of her condition while I look upon her—
Go mad! You had a daughter yesterday—
Brag of her now. "Point to her cheek, and ask
"If ever grew such smiles as blossom there!
"And bid the ear that listens to her, note
"The sweetness that it feasts on!" (*Music.*)
   Hark! thou'rt call'd!
What! not thro' the task thou hast begun
So bravely? Slay thy child, and finish it!
   [*Rushes out,* L. H.

Ina. (*Alone.*) They'd thwart a maid in her first love,
   they would!
They think it easy, but they'll find it hard!
When first they said I should become a bride,
Wondering how I would deck me, I ran thro'
The ranks of fairest flowers to pick me one
To set it in my bosom, and I remember
It was a rose I pitched on—there's the rose!
   (*Draws a dagger, and returns it to her
   bosom. Music.*)
The rites begin, I'll steal after them,
And watch the time! I'm coming to thee, Oswith!
I'll show thee how a Danish maid can love!
   [*Exit,* L. H.

SCENE II.—*Selwood Forest.* Enter *Oddune,* R. H.
   and Arnold, L. H., *meeting.*

   Od. No sign of Alfred?
   Arn. None! Our scouts have all
Return'd dishearten'd with their fruitless search.
   Od. Where can he linger—with so fair a wel-
   come
Impatient waiting him, as he would meet
From yonder gallant bands? The spirits now
That bear their crests so high, from his delay
To lead them on to action, will anon
Begin to droop—perchance may quite subside!
   Arn. How many do we muster?
   Od. By the last
Return, six thousand men.
   Arn. The field shows fair!
   Od. Fair cause—fair field! Who'd e'er expect so
   soon
To see the armour burnish'd up again
They cast aside for good! A pity 'twere
What shows such thrift should not be turn'd to
   use;
But, bootless, thrown away! They will not fight
Unless the king commands them!
   Arn. See, my lord,
What movement's that?
   Od. Here's one will tell us.
   Edg. (*Entering.*) Be
Prepared, my lord. The soldiers clamour for
The king, and doubts are spreading thro' the
   ranks;
You humour them—he will not come to lead
   them.
Their chiefs are hastening hither, from your own
   lips
Assurance to receive, and fair encouragement.

Enter EGBERT, KENRICK, ARTHUR, *Chiefs
   and Soldiers.*

   Eg. Now, Kenrick, speak! Say what the soldiers
   want.
   Od. Well, gallant friends! is England to be
   free?
Shall we change places with our conquerors,
Or still endure the yoke?
   Ken. We want the king!
Let him appear, we cannot meet the foe
Too soon!
   Od. As surely shall you see him, as
You long to see the foe!
   Ken. But when, my lord?
'Tis that we' know! When was the king the
   last
Upon the field? Has he not ever, on
The eve of battle, earlier than his chiefs,
Been out; with looks of ardour heartening us?
Our morning sun, that never clouded rose—
Enduing us with life and vigour new!
At most we muster bare six thousand men
To meet the Danish host! The king among us
Would make our numbers treble! Show us the
   king.
The only waving of his plume in battle
Were worth a hundred spears in hands as bold
As ever brandish'd weapon!
   Od. What, and if
Indeed he should not come? Ought you to feel
Your tyrant's feet upon your necks the less?
Your king is present in his cause! Be that
Your king!

   ALFRED *enters, still disguised.*
Whoever leads you, meet the Dane!
I speak not friends, because I'm next in place!
I care not for myself! Point out my post;
The van, the rear; I'll be content to take
My stand beside the man of meanest note
Among you! Make yon minstrel without helm
Or sword your leader, I will follow him!
So that I fight, I care not in what rank!
Let him who makes the absence of his king
Plea to desert his country and his king,
Fall off! So heaven sustain me in the cause,
Altho' our Alfred's presence now would add
Ten other richer lives to mine; yet say
He should not come, this faithful sword I draw
I will not sheath it till it has struck a blow
For liberty!
   Eg. I second you, brave Oddune.
   Arn. And so do I!
   Od. And so will every man,

Unless there be among the people one
That does not love his king!
 Ken. No, Oddune, no!
The people live but for their king!
 Alf. (Discovering himself.) The king
Lives only for his people! Oh! my people!
You are the drops of blood that make your king!
And do I see you once again in arms!
    (Bursts into tears. The chiefs and
      general soldiers seem affected.)
Oh friends! Why draw your hands across your
    eyes,
If mine should be asham'd of what they do?
We've met again, my friends! Who is the foe
Shall sunder us again? Oh, England! England!
Too fair—too richly gifted not to tempt
The spoiler—well that thou hast sons too true
To leave thee to his ravine! Thon'lt be free
Till thou art childless! Think not, gallant friends,
An hour I've squandered that was due to you,
And to our common country! I have seen
The Danish camp!
 Od. Their camp, my liege!
 Alf. Have stood
In Guthrum's very presence! That disguise
Will tell thee how. They'd fall an easy prey
To half our numbers! Friends! a royal stake
I've laid upon your heads that you will win
The day!
 Od. What stake, my liege?
 Alf. Your prince and queen!
They're in the spoiler's power. I might, indeed,
Have ransom'd them, but what he ask'd your king
    could not afford to pay.
 Od. What was't my liege?
 Alf. My people, Oddune.
 Eg. In the spoiler's power
Our prince and queen! What wait we for?
 Od. For nothing
But the king's word to move upon the foe!
 Alf. Upon him, then! Now think you on the
    things
You most do love! Husbands and fathers on
Their wives and children—lovers upon their
    mistresses—
And all upon their country! When you use
Your weapons, think on the beseeching eyes
To whet them could have lent you tears for water.
Oh, now be men or never! From your hearths
Thrust the unbidden feet, that from their nooks
Your aged fathers drove—your wives and babes!
The couches your fair-handed daughters us'd
To spread, let not the vaunting stranger press,
Weary from spoiling you! Your roofs that hear
The wanton riot of the intruding guest
That mocks their masters—clear them for the
    sake
Of the manhood, to which all that's precious
    clings
Else perishes. The land that bore you—oh!
Do honour to her! Let her glory in
Your breeding;—rescue her—revenge her, or
Ne'er call her mother more! Come on my friends!
And where you take your stand upon the field,
Thence, howsoever you advance, resolve
A foot you'll ne'er recede, while from the tongues
Of womanhood and childhood, helplessness
Invokes you to be strong! Come! Come on!
I'll bring you to the foe! And when you meet him
Strike hard! Strike home! Strike while a blow
Is in an arm! Strike till you're free, or fall!
    [Exeunt Alf. and the rest.

SCENE III.—*A wood. The statue of Odin in the centre; before it an altar prepared for sacrifice. Enter procession of sacrifice, in the following order:* —*Danish Chief with a body of Danish Soldiers; a body of Danish Chiefs, and* AMUND, EDRIC, *and* GUTHRUM; *a body of Danish Priests; Assistants with torches; Boys carrying censers; one Boy with a cushion, on which the knife of sacrifice is laid; Chief Priest of Odin;* OSWITH; *a body of Danish Soldiers. The procession marches to the following chorus:*—

Prepare the faggot—light the brand—
The victim's ready for the God!
The knife is bare in the sacred hand,
    That on the altar pours the blood!
        Prepare—prepare—prepare—
            Great Odin's rites—
        The mortal who slights,
His roof shall blaze in peace—his spear shall break in
    war!

 Guth. (L. H.) Saxon! Thou hast of life a moment
    yet
At thy command—use it for life—for love—
For liberty! But say the word, at once
The, weapon, ready for thy blood, is sheath'd,
Unstain'd and harmless!
 Os. I'm prepar'd to die!
 Priest. Saxon!
 Os. I come!
 Priest. Come! Bare his breast! Odin, receive thy
    victim!
 Ina. (*Rushing in,* 3 E. L. H.) Oswith I wed thee
    thus!
    (*She is on the point of plunging the
      dagger into her heart ; Oswith bursts
      from the Priest and arrests her arm.*)
 Os. Hold, Ina, hold!
Thou shalt not die with Oswith!
 Guth. Oswith, live!
Altho' the God himself demanded him,
He shall not die who saves my Ina's life!
 Priest. The servants of the God protect his
    rights!
 Oscar. (U. E. L. H. *Rushing in.*) The Saxon's in
    the camp, and down upon us!
 Alf. (*Without,* U. E. L. H.) Press on—press on—
    the first that comes to blows
Is the King's 'squire! Press on!
    (*The Danes front the stage on which the
      Saxons are coming, who enter, headed
      by Alfred. Danes are driven off;
      Alfred and Guthrum engage; Guth-
      rum is disarmed.*)

 Alf. Guthrum, live
The friend of Alfred! Serve the God he serves!
To wear a crown thou need'st not fight for one,
Except to keep it. Fair Northumbria
Receives thee for her King—my queen and son!
    (*Oddune leads on Elswith and Edith,* 2. E. R. H.)

    Enter EGBERT, *and* EDRIC *guarded.*

 Alf. Who's he?
 Eg. A traitor to our cause, my lord—
Whose sword has made more havoc 'mongst our
    people,
Than any ten of your foes! His hand, accurst!
It was that fir'd the hold where slept your queen
And son.

Ken and others. Dispatch him!
Alf. Hold! The victory
I will perpetuate by such an act
As shall from future king remove the power,
To make their public functions pander to
Their private gust. Select twelve men, his peers,
And swearing them upon the book of God,
As they shall answer at His judgment day,
To try their prisoner fairly. Let the charge
Be brought before them; and as they decide,
So finally his innocence or guilt
Establish'd! Hence! "Hereby shall private right,
" Which, guarded, fortifieth, more than arms,
" The conservator of the public weal,
" Be sacred even from the sceptre's touch!
" Thus to a people faithful to their king,
" A faithful king an institution gives
" That makes the lowly cottage lofty as
" The regal dome—holds justice paramount
" Of all—before her throne the peasant and
" The king himself on equal footing brings!
" A gift which you'll preserve for ever whole!
" From which, as from your blood, pollution keep!
" Which, if you're asked to render back, by all

" You owe yourselves, your country, and t'
throne,
" You'll answer no! Which, when you'd nam
you'll call
" Trial by Jury!"
Guth. Great the victory;
That kings gain o'er themselves. Blest are th
heads
That bow to sway like thine!
Alf. My countrymen!
Sons of the sea—henceforth her restless plain
Shall be your battlefield! There shall you meet
The threat'ning storm of war! There shall
burst
Its rage unfelt at home—its din unheard!
You've fought like England's true-born sons, t
day!
You've taught a lesson to her sons to come!
By your example fir'd, should e'er a foe
In after times invade her envied shores,
Her sons, of all descriptions and degrees,
To succour her shall grapple soul and hand,
Rampart her throne with living walls of hearts,
And teach the fell invader that the deep
Embrac'd her, never to betray her glory!

ADVERTISEMENTS.

MUSIC.

DICKS' PIANOFORTE TUTOR.

This book is full music size, and contains instructions and exercises, full of simplicity and melody, which will not weary the student in their study, thus rendering the work the best Pianoforte Guide ever issued. It contains as much matter as those tutors for which ten times the amount is charged. The work is printed on toned paper of superior quality, good and large type. Price One Shilling; post free, Twopence extra.

CZERNY'S STUDIES FOR THE PIANOFORTE.

These celebrated Studies in precision and velocity, for which the usual price has been Half-a-Guinea, is now issued at One Shilling; post free, threepence extra. Every student of the Pianoforte ought to possess this companion to the tutor to assist him at obtaining proficiency on the instrument.

DICKS' EDITION OF STANDARD OPERAS (full music size), with Italian, French, or German English Words. Now ready:—

DONIZETTI'S "LUCIA DI LAMMERMOOR," with Portrait and Memoir of the Composer. Price 2s. 6d. ROSSINI'S "IL BARBIERE," with Portrait and Memoir of the Composer. Price 2s. 6d. Elegantly bound in cloth, gilt lettered, 5s. each. Others are in the Press. Delivered carriage free for Eighteenpence extra per copy to any part of the United Kingdom.

REEVES' SIX CELEBRATED TENOR SONGS, Music and Words. Price One Shilling. Pilgrim of Love Bishop.—Death of Nelson. Braham.—Adelaide, Beethoven.—The Thorn. Shield. The Anchor's Weighed. Braham.—Tell me, Mary, how to Woo Thee. Hodson.

LINA PATTI'S SIX FAVOURITE SONGS, Music and Words. Price One Shilling. There be none of Beauty's Daughters. Mendelssohn.—Hark, hark, the Lark, Schubert.—Home, Sweet Home. Bishop.—The Last Rose of Summer. T. Moore.—Where the Bee Sucks. Dr. Arne.—Tell me, my Heart. Bishop.

CHARLES SANTLEY'S SIX POPULAR BARITONE SONGS. Music and Words. Price One Shilling. The Lads of the Village. Dibdin.—The Wanderer. Schubert.—In Childhood My Toys. Lortzing. Tom Bowling. Dibdin.—Rock'd in the Cradle of the Deep. Knight.—Mad Tom. Purcell.

*** Any of the above Songs can also be had separately, price Threepence each.

MUSICAL TREASURES.— Full Music size, price Fourpence. Now Publishing Weekly. A Complete Repertory of the best English and Foreign Music, ancient and modern, vocal and instrumental, solo and concerted, with critical and biographical annotations, for the pianoforte.

- Normandy (Ballad)
- Auld Robin Gray (Scotch Ballad)
- Sympathie Valse
- Pilgrim of Love (Romance)
- Pescatore (Song)
- Far-off Mountain (Duet)
- Anchor's Weigh'd (Ballad)
- Woman's Heart (Ballad)
- Mountain Home! (Duet)
- Wave, how Brightly Beams the Morning
- Marriage of the Roses (Valse)
- Emma (Duet)
- Heavenly Beauty (Cavatina)
- Childhood my Toys (Song)
- The Beauty Clothes the Fertile Vale
- Harp that once through Tara's Halls
- Manly Heart (Duet)
- Beethoven's "Andante and Variations"
- That Long-lost Home we Love (Song)
- Where the Bee Sucks (Song)
- Fair Dream ("Marta")
- Petit Fleur
- Angels ever Bright and Fair
- Light e'er should Sever (Duet)
- 'Tis but a little Faded Flow'r (Ballad)
- My Mother bids me Bind my Hair (Canzonet)
- Coming thro' the Rye (Song)
- Beautiful Isle of the Sea (Ballad)
- Tell me, my Heart (Song)
- How's Bank (Duet)
- The Minstrel Boy (Irish Melody)
- Hommage au Genie
- Oh what Pretty Brooms I've Bought
- Tom Bowling (Song)
- Tell me, Mary, how to Woo Thee (Ballad)

- 36 When the Swallows Homeward Fly (Song)
- 37 Rock'd in the Cradle of the Deep (Song)
- 38 Beethoven's Waltzes First Series
- 39 As it Fell upon a Day (Duet)
- 40 A Life on the Ocean Wave (Song)
- 41 Why are you Wandering here I pray? (Ballad)
- 42 A Maiden's Prayer.
- 43 Valse Brillante
- 44 Home, Sweet Home! (Song)
- 45 Oft in the Stilly Night (Song)
- 46 All's Well (Duet)
- 47 The "Crown Diamonds" Fantasia
- 48 Hear me, dear One (Serenade)
- 49 Youth and Love at the Helm (Barcarolle)
- 50 Adelaide Beethoven (Song)
- 51 The Death of Nelson (Song)
- 52 Hark, hark, the Lark
- 53 The Last Rose of Summer (Irish Melody)
- 54 The Thorn (Song)
- 55 The Lads of the Village (Song)
- 56 There be none of Beauty's Daughters (Song)
- 57 The Wanderer (Song)
- 58 I have Plucked the Fairest Flower
- 59 Bid Me Discourse (Song)
- 60 Fisher Maiden (Song)
- 61 Fair Agnes (Barcarolle)
- 62 How Calm and Bright (Song)
- 63 Woman's Inconstancy (Song)
- 64 Echo Duet
- 65 The Meeting of the Waters (Irish Melody)
- 66 Lo, Here the Gentle Lark
- 67 Beethoven's Waltzes (Second Series)
- 68 Child of Earth with the Golden Hair (Song)
- 69 Should he Upbraid (Song)

London: JOHN DICKS, 313, Strand; and all Booksellers.

ADVERTISEMENTS.

NOTICE TO THE PUBLI

One Penny Weekly,

DICKS' STANDARD P

A Play will be published weekly until further no

THE LADY OF LYONS. By Sir Edward Ly
WILD OATS. By John O'Keefe.
TOM AND JERRY. By W. T. Moncrieff.
OLIVER TWIST. By George Almar.
WOMAN'S WIT. By J. Sheridan Knowles.
"YES" AND "NO." (Two Farces in
C. A. Somerset and Francis Reynolds.
THE SEA-CAPTAIN. By Sir Edward Lytt
EUGENE ARAM. By W. T. Moncrieff.
THE WRECKER'S DAUGHTER. By
Knowles.
ALFRED THE GREAT. By J. Sheridan K
THE WANDERING MINSTREL and
(Two Plays in One Number.) By H. Mayhew
MY NEIGHBOUR'S WIFE and THE
BACHELOR. (Two Plays in One Number.)
and P. P. O'Callaghan.
RICHELIEU. By Lord Lytton.

Each Play will be printed from the Original Work of the Author, witho

To the Theatrical Profession, Amateurs, and others, this edition will as full stage directions, costumes, &c., are given. Remit penny stamp of upwards of three hundred.

London · JOHN DICKS, 313, Strand. All Newsagents

```
PR          Knowles, James Sheridan
4859           Alfred the Great
K5A5        Original complete ed.
1880
```

**PLEASE DO NOT REMOVE
CARDS OR SLIPS FROM THIS POCKET**

UNIVERSITY OF TORONTO LIBRARY

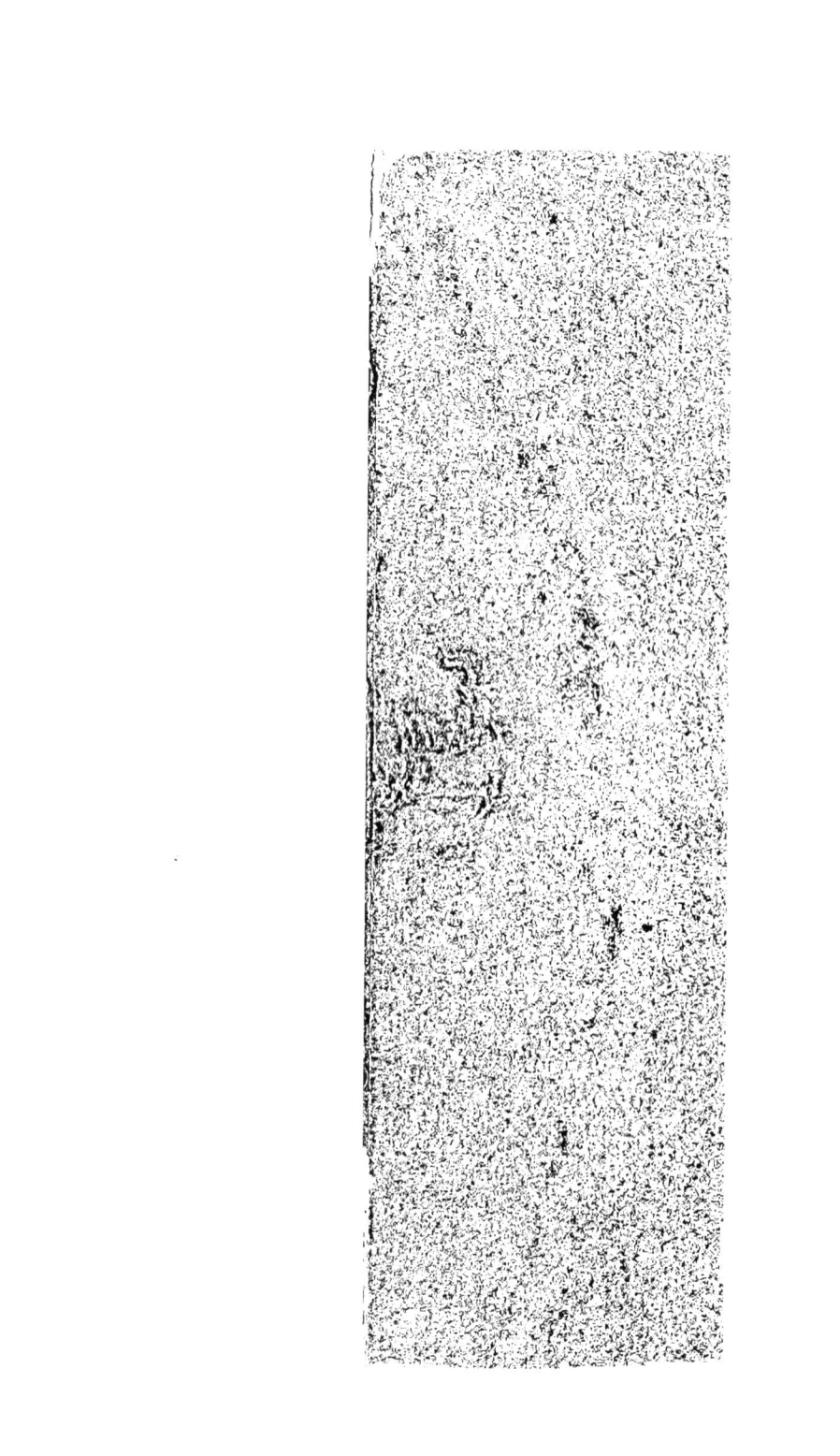

CPSIA information can be obtained
at www.ICGtesting.com
Printed in the USA
BVHW04*1054170918
527708BV00015B/2222/P